CW00693081

Ancient Egypt

An Enthralling Overview of Egyptian History, Starting from the Settlement of the Nile Valley through the Old, Middle, and New Kingdoms to the Death of Cleopatra VII

© Copyright 2023 - All rights reserved.

The content contained within this book may not be reproduced, duplicated, or transmitted without direct written permission from the author or the publisher.

Under no circumstances will any blame or legal responsibility be held against the publisher, or author, for any damages, reparation, or monetary loss due to the information contained within this book, either directly or indirectly.

Legal Notice:

This book is copyright protected. It is only for personal use. You cannot amend, distribute, sell, use, quote, or paraphrase any part, or the content within this book, without the consent of the author or publisher.

Disclaimer Notice:

Please note the information contained within this document is for educational and entertainment purposes only. All effort has been executed to present accurate, up-to-date, reliable, and complete information. No warranties of any kind are declared or implied. Readers acknowledge that the author is not engaging in the rendering of legal, financial, medical, or professional advice. The content within this book has been derived from various sources. Please consult a licensed professional before attempting any techniques outlined in this book.

By reading this document, the reader agrees that under no circumstances is the author responsible for any losses, direct or indirect, that are incurred as a result of the use of the information contained within this document, including, but not limited to, errors, omissions, or inaccuracies.

Free limited time bonus

Stop for a moment. We have a free bonus set up for you. The problem is this: we forget 90% of everything that we read after 7 days. Crazy fact, right? Here's the solution: we've created a printable, 1-page pdf summary for this book that you're reading now. All you have to do to get your free pdf summary is to go to the following website: **https://livetolearn.lpages.co/enthrallinghistory/**

Once you do, it will be intuitive. Enjoy, and thank you!

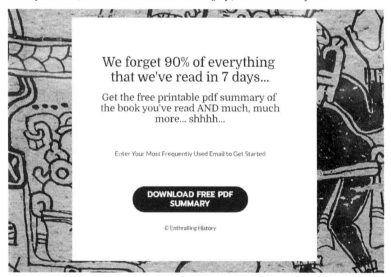

We forget 90% of everything that we've read in 7 days...

Get the free printable pdf summary of the book you've read AND much, much more... shhhh...

Enter Your Most Frequently Used Email to Get Started

DOWNLOAD FREE PDF SUMMARY

© Enthralling History

Table of Contents

Introduction

Long before the emergence of the first pharaoh, the Great Pyramids, hieroglyphs, and the towering obelisks was a land known by its people as Kemet. Literally translated as the "Black Land," the ancient name was believed to have been derived from the fertile yet pitch-black soil along the valley left by the Nile's annual inundation. While Kemet earned its name from the black soil, the natives also had another name for the deep reddish deserts; they called them Deshret or simply the "Red Land."

It was not until the birth of the ancient city of Memphis that its people began to refer to Kemet with a new name. Within the city was a temple called Hikuptah, which was dedicated to Ptah, the ancient god of craftsmen. The temple was so grand that it caught the attention of many, especially the Greeks. Upon learning about the prominence of the temple to the people of the Nile, the Greeks began to refer to the entire city as "Aigyptos," which was Greek for Hikuptah. From there on, the name became widely used by both natives of the land and foreigners. Eventually, Aigyptos was simplified to Egypt, the English spelling that we are all so familiar with today.

For many centuries, the ancient Egyptian civilization has managed to intrigue not only Egyptologists and scholars but also an array of other professionals, including writers, artists, and even architects from all over the world. The kingdom's impressive architectural designs and techniques have been studied over and over again just so we can uncover their secrets and apply them today, though the exact building technique of the pyramids was never entirely debunked until recently. The tales of the many pharaohs and stories of their battles are forever immortalized in books and movies, while the Egyptians' knowledge of astronomy and medicine was also greatly studied and used as a foundation by modern astronomers, medical practitioners, and scientists.

Whenever Egypt is mentioned, one cannot help but imagine the sight of the bleak and dry desert surrounding the pyramids, but have the lands of the Nile always been this way? Science tells us that due to the dramatic climate change that occurred at the beginning of the 4th millennium BCE, Egypt turned into a vast land full of life. The areas close to the Nile River were filled with lush vegetation, which attracted not only various species of animals but also the very first people who eventually set up seasonal camps and took shelter in the Nile Valley. Nabta Playa, a region of the Nubian Desert, for instance, was thought to have been wetter than today and was a site where one could find one of the earliest settlements in the ancient world. It was only after 3500 BCE that the valley witnessed another climate change, which led Egypt to gradually dry out and transform into the desert that we know today.

Being one of the earliest civilizations in the ancient world, it is definitely not a surprise that Egypt had gone through numerous changes, conflicts, disasters, and wars. The first unification of the kingdom thousands of years ago led to the rise of the Old Kingdom, a prosperous era that saw the construction of the pyramids, which are known by many. Perhaps the most flourishing era of Egypt was during the reign of the powerful pharaohs of the New Kingdom, which gave birth to the many impressive temples that survived the test of time.

However, although Egypt lasted for many centuries, it could not fully escape the dark times that terrorized the lands and its people. Famine, continuous political strife, constant warfare, and foreign invasions were some of the most common events that nearly crushed the kingdom. The Egyptians, led by the mighty god-like pharaohs, managed to overcome and repel the threats that could have engulfed their kingdom whole, but freedom was never meant to linger around the valley for too long.

In this book, you will not only get an insightful look into the early inhabitants of Egypt and the daily life of its people but also an enthralling journey of how the kingdom rose to power and eventually became desired by many foreign forces around the world. Jump from one pharaoh to another, reimagine their battles with other fierce forces beyond Egypt's borders, and dive deep into the unique Egyptian beliefs and traditions that held their people together.

Chapter 1: Settlers on the Nile I: Lower Egypt

Egypt, unsurprisingly, has its roots buried deep beneath the golden sands of the desert. The absence of written records caused scholars and historians alike to argue about when life first sprang across the Egyptian valley. After many series of excavations over the years, many agree that humans first occupied the region at least a millennium ago. Archaeologist Waldemar Chmielewski is believed to have discovered some of the oldest Egyptian structures near Wadi Halfa, a city in modern-day Sudan. These ancient structures, possibly a type of early Paleolithic dwelling, were estimated to date from 100,000 BCE. In the early 1980s, another excavation proved to be fruitful, as archaeologists discovered the Nazlet Khater skeleton, a complete set of human remains believed to have been over thirty thousand years old. With the success of the excavation and after several tests, experts could confidently conclude that Egypt had already gone through the Late Paleolithic period around 30,000 BCE.

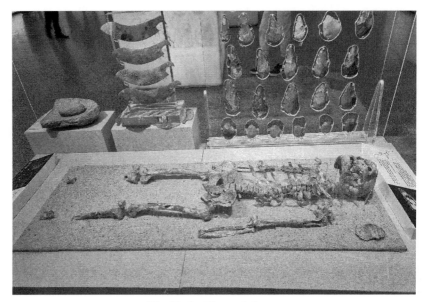

The Nazlet Khater skeleton.
Richard Mortel, CC BY 2.0 <https://creativecommons.org/licenses/by/2.0>, via Wikimedia Commons: https://commons.wikimedia.org/wiki/File:Nazlet_Khater_Skeleton.jpg

Though the traces of the past are largely visible in Egypt today, only a few of them can tell us the story of the Predynastic Period: a time when pyramids and pharaohs did not yet exist. Back then, Egypt was separated into two different lands: Lower Egypt, which was in the northern part of the Nile (the Nile runs south to north), and Upper Egypt in the south near the Sahara. Since these two separate lands had significant geographical differences, Egypt saw the birth of several different cultural eras, which were later named by experts after their respective Egyptian settlements.

Faiyum A Culture (c. 9000 BCE–6000 BCE)

During the Stone Age, Egyptians lived a rather simple life. They hunted big-game animals and collected berries and nuts. They did not even have permanent shelters. They often moved from one place to another, possibly to find better food sources and to escape from the impending dangers that nature holds. However, this lifestyle began to change as Egypt was ushered into the Late Neolithic period. The Egyptians began to resort to a semi-settled lifestyle.

With their knowledge of farming, which was acquired from the Levant, according to certain historians, the Egyptians built their new homes along the Nile, with some choosing the fertile lands of Faiyum. From what was once a barren desert basin with nothing in sight but dust and sand, Faiyum transformed into a lush oasis when the basin was filled with water from a branch of the Nile River. With new plants springing to life surrounding the oasis, several species of animals began to call Faiyum their new home, which eventually led to human beings occupying the area sometime around 9000 BCE.

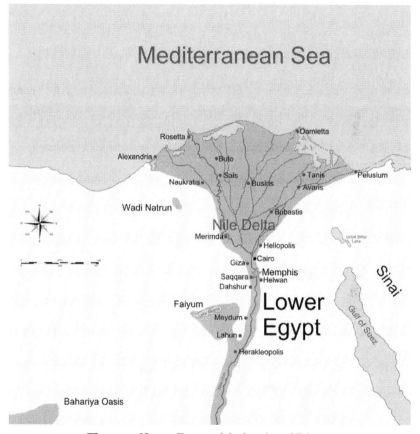

The map of Lower Egypt and the location of Faiyum.
Ancient_Egypt_map-en.svg: Jeff Dahlderivative work: MinisterForBadTimes, CC BY-SA 3.0 <https://creativecommons.org/licenses/by-sa/3.0>, via Wikimedia Commons: https://commons.wikimedia.org/wiki/File:Lower_Egypt-en.png

Since large cities were still thousands of years away from forming, these early Egyptians lived in small communities with only a few families. Seasonal camps with simple reed huts and mats were common in the Faiyum A culture, with the only permanent structures within their settlement being granaries and hearths. Pottery and tools of the Faiyum settlers, on the other hand, did not face any tremendous changes.

The three hundred ancient baskets, storage bins, and jars excavated from the surrounding area of this oasis town led experts to believe that Faiyum was, in fact, the birthplace of early Egyptian agriculture. Although Faiyum was not located on the banks of the Nile—the ancient town was approximately a hundred kilometers (sixty-two miles) away from Memphis (close to modern-day Cairo)—agricultural practices still thrived thanks to the river's annual flooding.

Typically, plants were cultivated in autumn, and harvests would be ready by spring. Since the crops relied heavily on the annual inundation, the harvests were not always guaranteed. The Egyptians could expect a terrible shortage of food supplies should the highlands of Ethiopia farther up the stream witness only little to zero rainfall. And so, to avoid such disaster, it could be plausible that the Egyptians moved to other locations in between the seasons, where they could hunt animals to further support their diets. However, once their crops were ready, they would return to Faiyum. These harvested crops, especially wheat and barley, were then collected in communal woven baskets, which were stored in close proximity to their settlement.

Merimde Culture (c. 5000 BCE–4200 BCE)

Over ninety years ago, the world was yet again surprised by another discovery. An expedition led by a German archaeologist named Hermann Junker uncovered another Egyptian neolithic culture up on the edge of the Western Delta. After sixteen years of excavations, the ancient settlement, also known as Merimde Beni Salama, went down in history as the earliest permanent settlement to ever exist in the Egyptian valley. Overlapping in time with the late period of the Faiyum A culture, the Merimde culture was believed to have been rather more advanced, despite sharing influences from both the people of Faiyum and the Levant. In fact, the settlement went through a total of three main cultural phases, each with its own characteristics, technology, and customs.

Like its predecessor, the early people of the Merimde culture were often described as primitive. They lived in small dwellings, which were typically flimsy and unrefined, while their ceramics were untempered; perhaps they preferred functionality over design. Occasionally, some were subtly decorated with a simple herringbone pattern. Agriculture was, of course, their main occupation from the beginning, although animal domestication and big-game hunting also played important roles in their daily lives. Goats, pigs, fish, turtles, crocodiles, and even hippopotami were some of the most common animals eaten by the Merimde people.

As Merimde entered its second cultural phase, the most evident advancement one could notice was the people's shelters. From simple huts, they evolved into sturdier dwellings with an oval-shaped ground plan. Given their larger spaces, these wooden houses often featured clay floors with hearths and a few storage jars. Even though only a little difference could be seen in their ceramic works—there were little to zero decorations—each piece appeared to be more polished and greatly refined. To sustain their diet, grain cultivation, fishing, and hunting activities continued, while animal domestication focused more on cattle.

The third and final phase, which many prefer to refer to as the Classic Merimde period, was a time when the people were beginning to take the first few steps to create a more organized community. Sticking to the previous oval-shaped ground plan, their houses were bigger and well constructed. Narrow streets occupied the spaces of the densely packed settlements. Each of the dwellings housed its own granaries, hearths, storage jars, and even grinding stones, which could possibly indicate that, in contrast to the Faiyum A culture, the families of the Merimde settlement were more independent, both socially and economically.

By the final phase of the Merimde culture, the ceramic works began to appear more intricate. The wares were often painted in a combination of deep red and black, with different types of engravings adorning the outer layers. This was also the time when human-like pottery first flourished. The cylindrical Merimde clay head, despite lacking realistic features, was believed to have been made as early as the 4th millennium BCE, thus making it the earliest known pottery representation of a human in ancient Egypt.

Without written records, it is hard for us to get a deep insight into the early beliefs and customs of the predynastic Egyptians.

However, the discovery of a few grave pits could suggest that the people of Merimde practiced a simple burial tradition. Since no children's graves have ever been found surrounding the settlement, some Egyptologists conclude that only adults received a proper burial, while the remains of deceased children were simply thrown into rubbish pits. However, this has been disputed by a few scholars, as some suggest that the lack of a child's grave within the settlement was due to the annual flood, which could have possibly washed them away entirely. Nevertheless, in contrast to the later burial customs of the ancient Egyptians, the people of Merimde did not bury their deceased with any grave goods or weapons.

Merimde Clay Head.
kairoinfo4u, CC BY-SA 2.0 <https://creativecommons.org/licenses/by-sa/2.0>, via Wikimedia Commons:
https://commons.wikimedia.org/wiki/File:Merimde_clay_head,_Predynastic_Period,_Maadi_Era,_4th_millennium_BCE.jpg

El-Omari Culture (c. 4000 BCE–3100 BCE)

The El-Omari culture was named after Amim El-Omari, an Egyptian mineralogist who first discovered the site of the settlement. Located about five kilometers north of Helwan, a city on the bank of the Nile on the opposite side of Memphis, the settlement has left us with very little information about its inhabitants and their characteristics. By the time the site was discovered, Egyptologists could only find clear remnants of pits and post holes, some of which could indicate that the people of El-Omari once lived in houses made of wattle and daub. Certain pieces of tools were also found that resembled those from the Merimde culture. From the discovery of the tools, it could be concluded that the inhabitants of El-Omari focused more on fishing and agriculture rather than desert hunting. Their pottery was rather polished and decorated with a red coating.

Although we might not be able to reimagine exactly how the people of El-Omari lived their daily lives, we can get insights into how they once buried the dead. In contrast to those from the Merimde culture, the inhabitants of El-Omari buried the deceased with grave goods, though the items were not at all elaborate; they were often buried with only a single pot. While the dead were usually buried close to their shelters, their bodies were placed in a specific position. The deceased were placed in shallow pits lying on their left side with their face facing the west. The reason behind this position is uncertain, but some scholars believe that it was possibly due to the direction where the sun sets.

Though many remains found within the settlement were buried the same, with only a pot placed by their feet, one grave appeared slightly different. This particular man was buried with a staff that closely resembles an early version of the Ames Sceptre, a type of ancient weapon typically used by later Egyptian kings and perhaps, at least according to ancient Egyptians, gods. This could signify that the man was probably an important figure within the settlement; perhaps he was some sort of leader or local chief.

Maadi Culture (c. 3900 BCE–3500 BCE)

Almost similar to the inhabitants of El-Omari, the villagers of the Maadi culture preferred agricultural activities rather than desert hunting. Various animal remains discovered at this ancient settlement indicate that animal domestication was the norm, with cattle, sheep, goats, and pigs being the most common animals in the village. The people of the Maadi culture were also the earliest to have domesticated donkeys, which were often used for trade. Aside from neighboring Upper Egypt, they were believed to have traded widely with people who lived in what today comprises Palestine. Through the many trade activities, the people of Maadi were able to import various resources. Copper, oil, and resin were imported from Palestine, while greywacke cosmetic palettes were obtained from Upper Egypt.

Only little remains of their dwellings, but we know they lived in oval huts made out of wood and matting. Both rectangular and subterranean structures were common within the settlement, with some bearing similarities with those discovered in the ancient city of Beersheba (located in modern-day southern Israel). It could also be plausible that the villagers stored their supplies communally since several jars and large pits were found at the end of the settlement. Contrary to the El-Omari culture, the Maadi pottery was rarely decorated; it was only painted black or red.

When it comes to burial customs, the villagers of Maadi laid the dead to rest in simple graves located in cemeteries away from the settlement. Only children and stillborn infants were believed to have been buried within the settlement. Since their pottery was rather simple and undecorated, burying the dead with grave goods was not a must for the people of the Maadi culture. Apart from humans, the villagers also had a designated cemetery for animals. However, not all animals were given proper burials since the graves were reserved for animals used in a sacrificial ceremony for a funerary cult.

Chapter 2: Settlers on the Nile
II: Upper Egypt

To say the people from the ancient world were brilliant is definitely an understatement. They were, indeed, far more advanced and ahead of their time. Nabta Playa, an archaeological site located in the Nubian Desert about a hundred kilometers away from Abu Simbel, is best known for portraying the excellent minds of the ancient people. The site contains the very first alignments of megaliths in the world. The ancient stone circle, thought to have been built at least seven thousand years ago, was accidentally discovered sometime in 1973 by a nomadic Arab guide. Believed by many to have been constructed by a group of nomadic people who once worshiped cattle, the megaliths were mainly used to determine the summer solstice and estimate the arrival of monsoons.

The reconstruction of the Nabta Playa stone circle at the Aswan Nubian Museum.
Raymbetz, CC BY-SA 3.0 <https://creativecommons.org/licenses/by-sa/3.0>, via Wikimedia Commons: https://commons.wikimedia.org/wiki/File:Calendar_aswan.JPG

Apart from the ancient megaliths, Nabta Playa was also considered one of the world's earliest settlements. Historians suggest the site welcomed its first inhabitants between eleven thousand and nine thousand years ago. Inhabited by a group of nomads, possibly of sub-Saharan African origin, the region was initially filled with only seasonal camps. As the centuries went by, Nabta Playa, like other prehistoric settlements in Egypt, witnessed gradual developments. From seasonal camps, the inhabitants began building more sophisticated huts and fire hearths, which were usually arranged in a straight line. The existence of gazelles and numerous wild plants growing around the area allowed the people to enjoy a more settled lifestyle. Later on, animal domestication became the norm; they usually raised goats and sheep.

The Badarian Culture (c. 4400 BCE–4000 BCE)

Named after its location at El-Badari, some two hundred kilometers away from the city of Thebes (modern-day Luxor), the Badarian culture mostly focused on agriculture. This settlement had the earliest evidence of agriculture in Upper Egypt. While the Badarian people often cultivated barley, wheat, herbs, and lentils to supplement their diet, they were also involved in fishing, animal domestication, and hunting, with gazelles being their main target.

Unfortunately, little is known about their dwellings, though the discovery of wooden stumps might suggest they once lived in simple and lightweight wooden huts; after all, they were semi-mobile. However, their burial practices were slightly complex, at least compared to the settlements found in Lower Egypt. In Badari, the deceased were wrapped in animal hides and placed on reed mats before getting buried in pits with their head facing west. The lack of battle wounds on the human remains discovered at the site also suggests the villagers of Badari were rather peaceful. Men were not buried with weapons, which possibly indicates that the Badarian people were not warriors.

Certain graves featured more than one grave good. Some were buried with a type of female mortuary statue, while there were also others that featured different personal items, such as shells, tools, jewelry made out of precious stones, and amulets carved in the shape of various animals, such as hippopotami and antelopes.

A Badarian female mortuary statue.
Louvre Museum, CC BY-SA 2.0 FR <https://creativecommons.org/licenses/by-sa/2.0/fr/deed.en>, via Wikimedia Commons:
https://commons.wikimedia.org/wiki/File:Woman-E_11887-IMG_9547-gradient.jpg

14

The people of this particular settlement were best known for their human-like sculptures and pottery. They were finely crafted and polished compared to the earlier periods. Some of the Badarian figurines became the foundation for later ancient Egyptian sculptures. The black-topped pottery, which made its first appearance in Nabta Playa, were commonly seen in this settlement, though they were often reserved for funerary and ritual purposes.

Historians and anthropologists have also suggested that the people of the Badarian culture were of the same racial mix as the ancient Egyptians of later dynasties. Egyptologist John Romer supported this claim by explaining the similarities of the Badarian people with the later ancient Egyptians. Their hair was either curly or straight and either light brown or black. Like the men of later periods, the Badarian people were mostly clean-shaven, while women often styled their hair in fringes and adorned it with combs made of either bone or ivory.

The Naqada Culture (c. 4000 BCE–3000 BCE)

The most important prehistoric culture of Upper Egypt is none other than the Naqada culture, which blossomed following the Badarian culture in 4500 BCE. Similar to the rest of the cultures discovered in the valley, the Naqada culture was also named after its location. This particular culture was divided into three different phases, each with its own unique characteristics and developments.

The earliest phase, Naqada I (also referred to as the Amratian phase), emerged concurrently with the Badarian culture, though it slowly replaced the latter as time passed. The people of Naqada I supplemented their diets by cultivating crops, and they lived in rather small villages. Their dwellings were more sophisticated. It is plausible that their houses featured windows and had walls made of wattle and daub. Despite appearing smaller in size, each of these villages had its own totems that represented its animal deity. The deities were possibly chosen according to their association with their clan or village.

However, the most prolific change was in terms of their sculptures and art. During this time, Naqada saw an increase in bearded male statues and sculptures of women, the latter of which were often associated with fertility. These statues were typically used for funerary purposes. Many graves of the Naqada culture featured at least one statuette, which served as company for the deceased in the underworld. This custom was practiced by later Egyptians. Food, pottery, jewelry, ornaments, weapons, and decorated palettes were some of the most popular items interred with the dead.

Sometime around 3,500 BCE, the second phase of the Naqada culture happened, which is known to us today as the Naqada II culture. The people of this culture no longer hunted animals as part of their daily activities since they had mastered the art of agriculture. The discovery of artificial irrigation during this period greatly aided their agricultural activities. The people of Naqada II went from living in small villages to building bigger towns and, later on, cities, which resulted in a booming population. Their houses also faced tremendous changes. They were constructed out of sunbaked bricks, and certain dwellings even had courtyards. Not to forget the dead, their graves also witnessed major changes. They were more ornate and expensive. The best example was found in Abydos (which later developed into a necropolis or a city of the dead), which contained a great number of massive and important tombs.

With their growing skills in architecture, they constructed palaces and temples. The oldest Egyptian temple built by them was in the city of Nekhen, better known as Hierakonpolis. This temple complex had its own courtyard and several small buildings, which later became a source of inspiration for an Old Kingdom pharaoh named Djoser when he constructed his famous Step Pyramid complex.

The final phase, the Naqada III culture, also referred to as the protodynastic period or Dynasty 0, was considered the most important part of Egypt's early history since this was the very culture that shaped the future Egyptian dynasties. During this period of time, Egypt had already seen the birth of many kings and rulers who claimed their holds over the divided kingdom. These rulers were usually named after animals related to their totems and were considered the personification of their gods—a belief that no doubt made its way into dynastic Egypt. In contrast to the rulers of Lower Egypt, who wore red crowns, those in Upper Egypt wore white crowns that resembled a bowling pin. Military campaigns were constantly launched, which eventually reduced the many city-states of Upper Egypt into only three: Thinis, Naqada, and Hierakonpolis

(Nekhen).

Hieroglyphs, which simply mean "the words of god," were believed to have originated during the earliest Naqada phase, though they continued to develop during the period of Naqada III. This form of writing was initially used only on pottery and acted as nothing but decoration. However, starting from 3200 BCE, hieroglyphs were used to keep important records, but no complete sentences were ever found originating from this period. The earliest record of complete hieroglyphs dates to the Second Dynasty.

The hieroglyphs, which were composed of a combination of logographic, syllabic, and alphabetic elements, were difficult to translate. However, thanks to the discovery of the Rosetta Stone in 1799, Egyptologists and scholars were able to decipher the ancient Egyptian language. Another form of writing introduced in Naqada III was serekh, which was used as royal crests to identify a ruler's name.

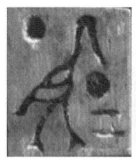

One of the earliest forms of Egyptian hieroglyphs.
https://commons.wikimedia.org/wiki/File:Design_of_the_Abydos_token_glyphs_dated_to_3400-3200_BCE.jpg

The royal serekh representing the first pharaoh of Egypt, Narmer.
https://commons.wikimedia.org/wiki/File:Narmer_Palette_verso_serekh.png

Many scholars agree that Mesopotamia played a significant role in the development of Egyptian civilization. Certain sculptures, ceramics, construction techniques, tomb designs, and even the early form of the ancient Egyptian religion could be traced back to Mesopotamian influences. This was probably due to the growing trade activities that took place around the kingdom. Egypt was believed to have made constant contact with not only Mesopotamia but also Canaan and Nubia.

Chapter 3: The Early Dynastic Period and the First Pharaoh

Before the age of mortal kings and pharaohs, the Egyptians believed their land was once ruled by a mythical king known as Osiris. Born shortly after the creation of the world, Osiris was made the lord of the earth and married his sister, Isis, who was the goddess of fertility, healing, and magic. The tradition of marrying siblings was widely practiced by the ancient Egyptians, typically among pharaohs and royals.

Osiris watched over his people but grew weary of their unfortunate state; they were rather primitive and uncivilized. And so, the compassionate god bestowed culture on them and introduced laws, agricultural activities, and religious practices to them. With his gifts and just reign, Egypt blossomed into a vast paradise where crops flourished and food supplies were plentiful.

Osiris, the god of the afterlife.

Eternal Space, CC BY-SA 4.0 <https://creativecommons.org/licenses/by-sa/4.0>, via Wikimedia Commons: https://commons.wikimedia.org/wiki/File:Osiris_(God).png

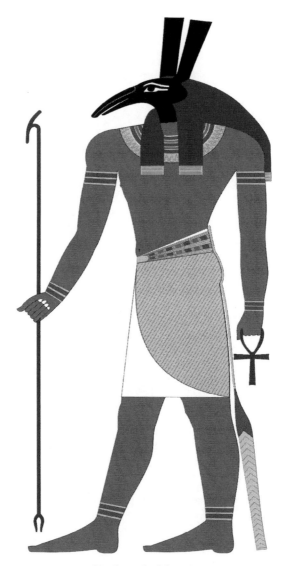

Set, the god of chaos.

Jeff Dahl (talk · contribs), CC BY-SA 4.0 <https://creativecommons.org/licenses/by-sa/4.0>, via Wikimedia Commons: https://commons.wikimedia.org/wiki/File:Set.svg

The Egyptians adored their king and queen since the people were treated fair and equally, no matter their status, age, wealth, or gender. While the royal pair were loved by many, one figure was hiding in the shadows, plotting to remove them from the throne and steal the crown for himself. This envious figure was Set, the god of chaos and the brother of Osiris.

Set eventually came up with a slow yet vicious plan to eradicate his brother. While hosting a grand banquet, Set presented his guests with a specially crafted chest or coffin, which he had secretly made to fit only Osiris. He then offered the intricate chest to whoever could fit into it, knowing full well that it could only fit his brother. The moment Osiris lay down in the chest, Set immediately sealed the lid and threw it into the Nile River. With the beloved king and god of Egypt gone, Set successfully realized his dreams. He was pharaoh.

Learning of her husband's terrible fate, Isis wept as the years passed by, leading to the flooding of the Nile. She managed to recover Osiris's remains; however, before she could attempt to resurrect the deceased god-king, Set arrived to put a stop to the plan. The god of chaos chopped the ice-cold remains of his brother before scattering the pieces to every corner of the world.

And so, Isis set on another journey to find and collect the pieces of Osiris so that she could bring him back to the land of the living. However, even the mightiest of gods could not escape their fate. Isis found all of Osiris's missing pieces except for one. Without the missing piece, he was only able to return to the living world for a short while. When his time was up, Osiris was left with no choice but to leave his dear wife and newborn son, Horus, to carry on with his new destiny as the lord of the underworld and judge of the dead. Heartbroken by the eternal departure of her husband and afraid of her son's future, Isis hid Horus somewhere in the isolated swampy marshland until he became old enough to fight for his right to the throne.

Golden statues of Horus (left), Osiris (middle), and Isis (right).
https://commons.wikimedia.org/wiki/File:Egypte_louvre_066.jpg

Under Set's reign, Egypt was plunged into mayhem, as the lands and the people were no longer united. Peace was a thing of the past. Seeing the chaos unleashed by Set and remembering his father's murder, a fully grown Horus challenged and battled Set. This struggle between the two gods was referred to as "The Contendings of Horus and Seth" (with Seth being a common variant of Set). In the end, Horus, who was proved to be the mightier warrior, successfully defeated Set. While some claimed the god of chaos was killed by his nephew, many suggest that he was, in fact, spared but driven out of the land.

With the chaos finally conquered by Horus, Egypt was reunited again. Order was restored, and the people welcomed Horus as their new king, thus marking the beginning of another prosperous era in Egypt.

Although the story of Set's demise and Horus's rise to the throne is nothing short of a myth that survived thousands of years, several researchers and Egyptologists agree that the myth was, believe it or not, created to mirror the historical unification of Egypt sometime around 3150 BCE. Since the Egyptians were a step closer to becoming more civilized, the two lands—Upper and Lower Egypt— witnessed an increasing number of wars and battles between the different settlements and villages. That was, however, until a king of Upper Egypt made a move to change the course of history and finally unite the two separate kingdoms.

Before the discovery of thousands of artifacts that tells us the story of Egypt's unification, scholars and historians depended on the *Aegyptiaca* (*History of Egypt*), a collection of three history books authored by a man known as Manetho. Nothing is known about Manetho except that he was a priest living in Sebennytos (modern-day Samannud) during Egypt's Thirtieth Dynasty. His works, which were originally commissioned by the second king of the Ptolemaic dynasty, Ptolemy II, consist of a long chronological list of the kings who once reigned over ancient Egypt, from the mythical god-kings of the earliest of times to the very first pharaoh who wore both crowns of Upper and Lower Egypt to the establishment of the New Kingdom.

According to Manetho, Egypt was united by a certain king who went by the name of Menes. Considered the first human king of Egypt by some ancient Egyptians, Menes was often credited with the successful conquest of the Nile Delta and the establishment of Memphis, the glorious city that stood on the border between Upper and Lower Egypt. He was believed to have ruled the two parts of Egypt for over sixty years until he was killed by a hippopotamus. However, whether Menes was merely a legendary figure or the first king of a unified Egypt has been disputed by many due to the lack of archaeological evidence.

This can be seen when British archaeologists James E. Quibell and Frederick W. Green discovered the Narmer Palette in the late

19th century. The palette, which had survived over five millennia in almost perfect condition, contains the earliest example of hieroglyphic inscriptions that depict the scenes of Egypt's unification. However, the inscriptions left historians and scholars with more questions rather than a clear answer; the name of the king on the palette credited with uniting Egypt was not Menes but a figure named Narmer.

Narmer was believed to have initially ruled over Upper Egypt, with his seat being in Thinis. The king, who was completely aware of the need to form a strong army for his unification campaign, gathered the many tribal leaders across his regions, thus forming a confederacy. With the tribes in tow, Narmer was able to march toward the north and launch his invasion, which resulted in the defeat of Lower Egypt. With zero opposition standing in his way, Narmer successfully united the lands of the Nile, crowning himself as the first pharaoh of Lower and Upper Egypt in the process.

The Narmer Palette, depicting Narmer in the Hedjet, the white crown of Upper Egypt subjugating his enemy.
Heagy1, CC BY-SA 3.0 <https://creativecommons.org/licenses/by-sa/3.0>, via Wikimedia Commons: https://commons.wikimedia.org/wiki/File:Narmer_Palette_verso.jpg

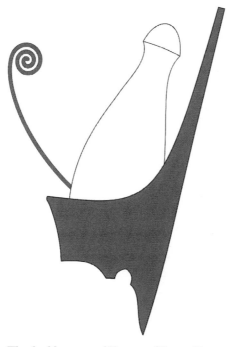

The double crown of Upper and Lower Egypt.

Jeff Dahl, CC BY-SA 4.0 <https://creativecommons.org/licenses/by-sa/4.0>, via Wikimedia Commons: https://commons.wikimedia.org/wiki/File:Double_crown.svg

For quite some time, scholars agreed that the two kings were two different individuals. Narmer was thought to have peacefully unified the two kingdoms at the end of the Predynastic Period, while Menes was his successor who continued to unify the region through conquest, thus kickstarting Egypt's Early Dynastic Period. With more archaeological evidence, however, this view began to change. The Egyptologist Flinders Petrie finally put the debate to rest by suggesting that Narmer was the name of Egypt's first pharaoh while Menes was his honorific.

Many historians agree that Narmer was married to a woman named Neithhotep, with whom he had a child. And so, when it was high time for the Egyptian throne to welcome a new ruler, his son, who went by the name of Hor-Aha, took over his father's legacy and ruled over the unified kingdom. Similar to his father, not much is known about Hor-Aha. Certain sources even claimed that Hor-Aha was, in fact, Menes himself; however, the discovery of the seals bearing his name that identified him as the second pharaoh of the dynasty contradicts the claim. Nevertheless, we can conclude that Hor-Aha was once a religious ruler. Tablets originating from his reign seem to describe his visit to the shrine of the goddess Neith, possibly to perform a ritual or important religious activity. Aside from the tablets, the discovery of a few intricate items, such as ivory boxes, white marble, and finely carved copper axes, also suggests the quality of craftsmanship across the kingdom had greatly improved during the time of Hor-Aha. The second king of the First Dynasty was also said to have led expeditions into Nubia. However, compared to his father's rule, trade activities, especially with the southern Levant, did not fare so well under his reign.

Hor-Aha was succeeded by his son, Djer, about whom we know almost nothing. According to the inscriptions on the Palermo Stone, the king ruled for nearly forty years and was said to have launched a campaign to an unspecified land somewhere in southern Canaan. The specifics of this campaign and the rest of his reign are forever lost to us since the Palermo Stone was heavily damaged. Though not enough details survived the time that could tell us more about his reign, his death has given us great insight into ancient burial customs and traditions of the Egyptians, especially the kings. Surrounding his tomb in Abydos, archaeologists discovered at least three hundred subsidiary graves, which belonged to the members of the court, the royal family, and possibly the king's most loyal servants. They were thought to have been sacrificed and buried alongside the king. The Egyptians believed that after death, these people would rise and join their king in the next world.

After Djer's death, Egypt saw the rise of many new kings who would continue to lay the foundations of a booming civilization. Over a period of a few centuries, the Nile kingdom went through gradual changes. More local districts established new trade networks that further led to Egypt's flourishing economy. Agricultural activities were done on a larger scale than before, and the Egyptian writing system also saw tremendous growth.

Chapter 4: Pyramids, Gods, and Pharaohs: The Rise of the Old Kingdom

The Egyptian civilization continued to flourish after the unification of the lands. Settlements turned into towns, and cities began to see the birth of dozens of glorious monuments, temples, and statues. Most of them were dedicated to their pharaohs (or kings since the term "pharaoh" only began to be used in the New Kingdom) and the ancient gods and goddesses who were thought to have blessed the people with gifts and protection in life and death. Although the gods were believed by the ancient Egyptians to have had their eyes on all of their subjects, most of the time, only the mighty pharaoh could communicate with them. The first king of the Third Dynasty, Djoser, was said to have saved Egypt from famine following a conversation with a god in his dream.

The Famine Stele of Djoser.
Morburre, CC BY-SA 3.0 <https://creativecommons.org/licenses/by-sa/3.0>, via Wikimedia Commons: https://commons.wikimedia.org/wiki/File:Sehel-steleFamine.jpg

According to the Famine Stele, the people of Egypt were terrorized by a terrible famine and drought that lasted for nearly seven consecutive years. The farmlands were left with no harvests. Grains were scarce, and kernels dried up when the annual flooding of the Nile failed to come. Hundreds of families suffered, with death and starvation becoming the norm across the valley. Some succumbed to their fate without protests, while many others began to break the laws in desperation. Farmers turned into robbers, and priests were left with no choice but to return to their homes since temples and shrines were closed down.

Seeing the chaos gradually devouring his subjects—possibly at the behest of Set, the god of destruction and chaos—Djoser grew wary and decided to consult his chancellor and the high priest of Ra, Imhotep. Since no one had even the slightest idea of how to overcome the drought, the king asked Imhotep to leave the safe walls of Memphis and go on a journey to find the ancient god who had the power to control the Nile. With haste, Imhotep traveled to Hermopolis, where he began his investigation by reading a series of archives from the city's temple. There, he discovered that the flooding of the Nile was controlled by a god named Khnum.

Imhotep returned to Memphis and presented his findings to the pharaoh, who later thanked him. Following the meeting with his chancellor, Djoser was visited by the god Khnum himself in a dream; some sources claim that it was Imhotep who dreamt of the god. Nevertheless, the kind-looking god informed the pharaoh of an abandoned temple on the island of Elephantine. Khnum claimed the Egyptians no longer respected the gods, especially the one who gave them life through the river.

Waking up from his unusual dream, Djoser consulted with Imhotep and another one of his governors, both of whom suggested that the pharaoh set sail to the island and see about the temple. Agreeing to the suggestion, Djoser traveled to the island of Elephantine. Just as his dream had foretold, the pharaoh discovered the dilapidated temple described by Khnum a few nights before. In an effort to pay his respects to the god, Djoser ordered his priests and people to restore the temple and issued a decree in which regular offerings were to be made to Khnum. When the reconstruction of the temple was completed, and the Egyptians resumed their offerings to the god, Khnum was pleased, resulting in the end of the seven-year-long drought and famine.

King Djoser: His Capital City, Expeditions, and Architectural Contributions

A limestone statue of Pharaoh Djoser.
Jon Bodsworth, Copyrighted free use, via Wikimedia Commons;
https://commons.wikimedia.org/wiki/File:Djoser_statue.jpg

Although already being hailed as the hero of Egypt by his people, Djoser continued to add more titles and honors to his name. Very little is known about his early years except that he was probably the son of the last king of the Second Dynasty, Khasekhemwy. Djoser had a wife named Hetephernebti, who was also his half-sister. The king was also known for moving the capital to Memphis.

Also referred to by the Egyptians as "Men-nefer" (which simply means "the enduring and beautiful"), Memphis was believed to have been secured by great white walls that gleamed under the scorching sun. The city was filled with monuments, markets, and grand religious temples that drew pilgrims and foreigners. Thanks to the continuous constructions and developments commissioned by Djoser and his successors, Memphis became ancient Egypt's most important cultural and commercial center. While the Egyptian cities were already beginning to blossom as early as the First Dynasty, by the reign of Djoser, they began to appear more intricate and complex.

The country learned the meaning of peace and harmony right after the unification of the two kingdoms by Narmer; however, wars were never fully resolved, especially outside of Egypt's borders. During Djoser's reign, one of his first goals was to strengthen the borders. With his country secured, the king then moved on to the next step: extending the borders of Egypt. Through carefully planned military expeditions, the king expanded his power over the region of Sinai, thus giving the Egyptians a way to mine precious minerals, such as copper and turquoise, from the area. Under the king's orders, the Egyptian military clashed swords with the Libyans and easily annexed certain parts of their land. Just like that, Djoser gained another honor to his name and was remembered by many.

However, Djoser's greatest contribution to ancient Egypt was not his successful military expeditions or even how he miraculously overcame the drought and famine. As soon as Djoser claimed the throne of Egypt, he showcased his fondness for architecture and design by commissioning the construction of a wide collection of structures and buildings in the city, including the very first pyramid of Egypt.

In Saqqara, northwest of glimmering Memphis, lies Djoser's proudest creation: the Pyramid of Djoser, which is also referred to as the Step Pyramid of Djoser. The pyramid was commissioned by the king at least 4,700 years ago in an attempt to set new standards for the burial rites of an Egyptian pharaoh. Before the pyramids, kings and royals were buried in rectangular tombs made out of mud slabs known as mastabas. These simple tombs were typically built above underground chambers and rose only six meters in height.

An example of a mastaba.
Jon Bodsworth, Copyrighted free use, via Wikimedia Commons;
https://commons.wikimedia.org/wiki/File:Mastaba-faraoun-3.jpg

Djoser's Step Pyramid, which was believed to have been Imhotep's idea (Imhotep was later deified by the ancient Egyptians and immortalized by historians), was the tallest structure to ever exist during that time. The pyramid, which consists of six mastabas stacked on top of each other, stood over sixty meters (almost two hundred feet) tall and was surrounded by a temple, courtyards, shrines, and living quarters built specifically for priests. In contrast to the earlier mastabas, this pyramid was made entirely out of limestone blocks.

Pyramid of Djoser.
Olaf Tausch, CC BY 3.0 <https://creativecommons.org/licenses/by/3.0>, via Wikimedia
Commons: https://commons.wikimedia.org/wiki/File:Sakkara_01.jpg

The reason behind the pyramid's height and all of the ornate images, statues, and symbols carved on the walls and columns vary. While some suggest that it was merely for the sake of inspiring awe, others claim their purpose was to assist the soul of the deceased. In ancient Egyptian beliefs, the souls of the rulers were thought to have the ability to fly from the heavens to earth. So, it was necessary for the deceased to be buried in a significant structure so that their souls could easily recognize their resting place from high above. That way, they would be able to visit the earthly plane and watch over their people once again.

No exact details of the pyramid's construction survived, but historians and archaeologists believe that the pyramid took years to complete, even with the help of hundreds of skilled craftsmen. However, we can be sure that the pyramid was once the resting place of King Djoser. The maze of tunnels underneath the base of the pyramid was designed to confuse and discourage grave robbers from getting their hands on the precious grave goods and the king's remains. Djoser's granite burial chamber was not the only room within the pyramid; there was also a ceremonial chamber built for the deceased pharaoh's soul. Unfortunately, the complex maze tunnels did not stop the grave robbers from finding their way in since Djoser's remains have been lost, along with most of the grave goods. What remains to this day is his Step Pyramid and some of his deeds carved onto the structures around the complex, which serve as a testimony to his prosperous reign.

Sneferu and the First True Pyramid

Sneferu was the first king of the Fourth Dynasty. He ruled over the vast kingdom for nearly twenty-four years. Thought by many to have been responsible for bringing Egypt much wealth and stability, the pharaoh was popularly known for his effort in perfecting the building of pyramids. To finance his construction programs, Sneferu turned to military expeditions. The pharaoh launched campaigns into the lands of Nubia and Libya. Aside from increasing the supplies of raw materials, Sneferu also looked to increase Egypt's labor force. Sources claim that due to the success of his raids, the pharaoh managed to get his hands on a great number of captives, who would later be put to work in the construction sites of his pyramids.

A relief of Sneferu in his funerary temple of Dahshur.

Juan R. Lazaro, CC BY 2.0 <https://creativecommons.org/licenses/by/2.0>, via Wikimedia Commons: https://commons.wikimedia.org/wiki/File:Snefru_hed-seb_festival.jpg

His reign is thought to have been a period of experimentation since he had numerous builders constructing various structures using an array of techniques. The discovery of different painting techniques on the tomb walls clearly indicates the Egyptians were experimenting to find the best ways to preserve images and inscriptions.

Sneferu's first pyramid, known as the Meidum Pyramid, can be found at Dahshur. The complex featured courtyards, temples, and a cult pyramid that was used as a place of worship for the pharaoh's funerary cult. Initially designed as a step pyramid, the pharaoh had his builders transform the structure into almost a true pyramid, making it the first pyramid with straight sides.

Sneferu's second pyramid, which is known to us today as the Bent Pyramid, also stood in Dahshur. Just as its name suggests, this pyramid was unlike any other since it appeared crooked. The reason behind this design was probably accidental; the unstable and sandy ground beneath the base of the pyramid left the builders with no other choice but to improvise the slope just so they could prevent the structure from collapsing.

His third and last pyramid, also known as the Red Pyramid, was considered his best. Consisting of 160 layers of stone, the Red Pyramid was Sneferu's first successful true pyramid, complete with a full limestone casing. This pyramid also went on to become the blueprint for the Great Pyramids of Giza. It is also the fourth-tallest surviving pyramid in Egypt today.

The Meidum Pyramid.
https://commons.wikimedia.org/wiki/File:Meidoum_pyramide_003.JPG

The Bent Pyramid.
*Ivrienen at English Wikipedia, CC BY 3.0 <https://creativecommons.org/licenses/by/3.0>,
via Wikimedia Commons:
https://commons.wikimedia.org/wiki/File:Snefru%27s_Bent_Pyramid_in_Dahshur.jpg*

The Red Pyramid of Sneferu.
*Hajor, CC BY-SA 1.0 <https://creativecommons.org/licenses/by-sa/1.0>, via Wikimedia
Commons: https://commons.wikimedia.org/wiki/File:Egypt.Dashur.RedPyramid.01.jpg*

The Pyramids of Giza

Perhaps following in the footsteps of his father, Khufu initiated the construction of his resting place shortly after his succession to the throne in 2575 BCE. He put his trust in his architect, Hemiunu, who told the pharaoh that he needed at least two decades to finish the pyramid. An unthinkable amount of limestone and granite was needed, and Hemiunu was also believed to have dug over six kilometers of a canal before he could even start constructing the pyramid's foundation.

The enormous building project required the energy of twenty-five thousand laborers. However, contrary to popular belief, these construction workers were not all enslaved people or captives of war. In fact, Egypt had its own labor supply; Egyptians were obligated to perform work for the government throughout the year. These builders were not only tasked to move and arrange the massive limestone blocks for ten hours every day, but they were also responsible for crafting the tools they needed for the work, as well as administrative tasks. The Egyptian government prepared houses and food for the workers. Some sources claim that those who worked on the pyramid lived a better life compared to the average citizen.

The Great Pyramid of Giza.
Nina at the Norwegian bokmål language Wikipedia, CC BY-SA 3.0
<http://creativecommons.org/licenses/by-sa/3.0/>, via Wikimedia Commons:
https://commons.wikimedia.org/wiki/File:Kheops-Pyramid.jpg

The construction process of the pyramid was rather complicated; one minor error at the base of the pyramid could result in a terrible failure at the top. Though historians and archaeologists today have discovered where the Egyptians obtained the materials needed to build the colossal structure—the stones were quarried from a site in Giza while the limestone casing was obtained from Tura, ancient Egypt's main limestone quarry right across the Nile—no one is able to determine the exact process of its construction. Upon completion, it was estimated that the pyramid was made of 2.3 million blocks of limestone, each weighing from 2.5 to 15 tons.

The remains of the limestone casing on the side of the pyramid.
Jon Bodsworth, Copyrighted free use, via Wikimedia Commons;
https://commons.wikimedia.org/wiki/File:Cheops_pyramid_02.jpg

The second pyramid of Giza was built by Khufu's son, Khafre, sometime in 2520 BCE. While Khufu's Great Pyramid was named the largest and tallest structure in Egypt at the time, the Pyramid of Khafre's most prominent feature was the mysterious limestone statue called the Sphinx. Like Khufu's pyramid, the outer part of the Pyramid of Khafre was once coated with limestone cladding, making it glimmer under the sun. On the apex of the pyramids, one could find a golden capstone, which sources claim would shine brightly even under the night sky.

About three decades after the construction of Khafre's pyramid, the complex saw the birth of the third and last tomb. The pyramid was considerably smaller than the other two and was built for Pharaoh Menkaure, Khafre's son. Despite its size, the pyramid had a more complex temple compared to both of its predecessors.

Chapter 5: The First Intermediate Period: Thebes, Memphis, and Herakleopolis

Among their many beliefs and ideologies, the ancient Egyptians believed that their rulers or pharaohs were the true embodiment of peace, justice, and divinity. (Most pharaohs were male, although there were a few female pharaohs.) Once crowned as the ruler of Egypt, the fate of the kingdom rested on their shoulders. Pharaohs had to oversee their realm with the blessings of the gods. Omens and signs were not to be taken lightly since they were considered messages from powerful deities. The rulers were expected to lead religious events and military campaigns against foreign powers beyond the borders of Egypt. They also had to oversee their subjects' welfare without rest and feed them during difficult times while ensuring justice in courts and trials.

Indeed, a pharaoh's power over the lands of the Nile was supreme, but even the divine ruler needed support to ensure Egypt never fell into chaos. Next in the hierarchy was the pharaoh's vizier, a high-ranking position within the government similar to a modern-day prime minister. Initially, the position could only be filled by a member of the royal family. However, by the Sixth Dynasty, pharaohs would typically appoint an individual based on their loyalty and attributes. Aside from being the bearer of the pharaoh's seal, viziers were also tasked with trade records, the government treasury, central granaries, state archives, and even the construction of monuments and structures across the valley. A vizier was supported by nomarchs. As king-appointed governors, the nomarchs were the ones expected to keep the Egyptian nomes or provinces under control.

Some of the government officials acted as the pharaoh's strongest supporters. Although they were given the power to oversee certain aspects of the government, they had to do so with the pharaoh's blessing. That was, however, until the decline of the Old Kingdom. Right after the death of Pepi II, Egypt saw the first signs of a decentralized government, as the nomarchs grew in power and eventually reversed Narmer's efforts. The kingdom was yet again divided.

While many would suggest that the Old Kingdom began to crumble at the end of Pepi II's reign, others claim that the signs were already visible before the pharaoh was even crowned. It started when the fourth king of the Sixth Dynasty, Pepi I, unknowingly bestowed more power and influence on the nomarchs. He first married two daughters of a nomarch and made their brother a vizier. Years later, Pepi II granted even more power to these provincial officials, perhaps because he was in need of more support due to his long years of reigning and old age. However, this move caused them to not only hold more influence over the people of the Nile but also led them to grow extremely wealthy. The nomarchs had a luxurious lifestyle, especially when they were exempted from taxes. They lived in opulent palaces, owned massive estates, and were fully protected by their own army. In death, they were put to rest in elaborate tombs.

To make matters worse, Pepi II appointed two viziers in his court instead of one. One of them was sent to Upper Egypt to oversee all official matters on the king's behalf, while the other gained power over Lower Egypt. This was a decision that no doubt contributed to the kingdom's division in the First Intermediate Period that followed.

Taking the mantle of kingship when he was just a child, Pepi II ruled Egypt for about ninety-six years—some suggest sixty-four years—making him the longest monarch to ever sit on the throne.

The pharaoh died sometime in 2184 BCE and left Egypt in turmoil. His son, Merenre II, who was quite old, took the throne. However, it is plausible that his power was only limited to the capital city. By this time, many believed the kingdom was beyond saving, as the increasing power of the nomarchs had put a crack in the central government, thus shaking the pharaoh's authority.

As the kingdom entered the First Intermediate Period (an era that is classified by many as Egypt's dark age), its people continued to fear for their future since chaos or *isfet* was clearly on the horizon. The land witnessed more than one individual who claimed to be the ruler of the vast valley, which was a huge sign of instability. According to Manetho, during the Seventh Dynasty, Egypt was ruled by seventy different kings in the span of seventy years. However, this was most likely a metaphor to describe the kingdom's fragmented state.

Just like the Seventh Dynasty, the next line of rulers (the Eighth Dynasty) left us with only scarce evidence. Not much has been discovered about their reigns except that they had only little to zero power in the kingdom. The lands were almost entirely ruled by the nomarchs who, at times, would wage war among each other and coerce the inhabitants of other nomes to accept their reign. Having different overlords, the fate of the Egyptians was rather uncertain. Those who resided within a nome governed by a reckless nomarch would face multiple challenges. Those who were fortunate enough to be put under a considerate nomarch had better chances to fall asleep at night. One nomarch who went by the name of Ankhtifi was said to have cared for his nome responsibly. According to his autobiographical inscription, the nomarch was believed to have eradicated the famine that plagued his people by supplying grain to the people.

While the power-hungry nomarchs attempted to grow their power, Herakleopolis, a city in Lower Egypt, saw the emergence of an individual who proclaimed himself to be the new pharaoh of Egypt. His name was Meryibre Khety I, the founder of Egypt's Ninth Dynasty, which is also referred to as the House of Khety. Despite having the title of king, Khety was never favored by his subjects. Manetho claimed that the king was the worst of them all. Violence was his answer to everything, and those who refused to acknowledge him faced a fate even worse than death. His cruel reign was thought to be despised by the gods, as the king soon turned mad and died (he was apparently eaten by a crocodile).

The House of Khety continued to claim themselves as kings, although their power was not enough to put a stop to the ruling nomarchs. Sources claim there were also times when they struggled with those who lived within Herakleopolis. The House of Khety was said to have been forced to deal with the rise of the Tenth Dynasty for nearly a decade until they could finally suppress them once and for all, thus permanently severing their plans to take over the throne.

Outside of Herakleopolis, Ankhtifi was gaining prominence. Despite claiming to have served the king from Herakleopolis, Ankhtifi had an ambitious plan to expand his power over the kingdom, specifically the southern territories of Egypt. So, he worked to gain control over two nomes in the south before moving on to take over the cities of Thebes and Gebtu. However, his attempt was unsuccessful when the two cities formed an alliance to repel his attack. The squabble between the two factions took a couple of years. Ultimately, Ankhtifi was defeated, resulting in Thebes taking control of the nomes held by the ambitious nomarch. With the end of the conflict, Thebes saw the birth of the Eleventh Dynasty, which was founded by an individual named Intef I. By proclaiming himself as both the king of Egypt and the son of Ra, Intef officially initiated a war with the neighboring ruler of Herakleopolis.

Conflicts between the two rival kings went on for years, beginning from the reign of Intef I up until his successors, Intef II and Intef III. By the time of Theban Pharaoh Mentuhotep II's reign, Egypt was beginning to witness clear signs of unification. Although having control over both Lower and Middle Egypt, the kings of Herakleopolis soon signed their own death warrants when they damaged the royal necropolis of Abydos. Without hesitation, Mentuhotep II dispatched his troops to the north, where they laid an attack on the city of Herakleopolis itself. The Theban king and his armies swiftly defeated the enemy garrison and immediately wasted the city. Those who opposed them were slaughtered, and the many tombs belonging to the royal families were desecrated.

The fate of his rival, the king of Herakleopolis, remains a mystery, but we can be sure that Mentuhotep achieved a great victory during this battle and was made the sole ruler of Egypt, thus unifying the kingdom and kickstarted the flourishing Middle Kingdom.

A relief of Mentuhotep II.
https://commons.wikimedia.org/wiki/File:MentuhotepII.jpg

Learning from the mistakes made by the last rulers of the Old Kingdom, which led to Egypt's decentralization of power, Mentuhotep immediately reformed the kingdom's governing system. He limited the powers of the nomarchs and established a set of new government positions, which were later given to only his most loyal men. Government officials from the capital were encouraged to regularly visit the many territories of Egypt just so they could keep a close eye on the regional leaders.

Aside from launching campaigns beyond the borders of Egypt and strengthening the kingdom's name in the eyes of foreign powers, Mentuhotep II also focused on the construction of many temples throughout the valley, though few of his works survived. His biggest building project was none other than his large mortuary temple, which later became a huge inspiration for a pharaoh of the New Kingdom, Hatshepsut.

Chapter 6: Egypt Unified: Rise of the Middle Kingdom

The unification of Egypt might have been credited to Mentuhotep II, but the kingdom was not completely free from chaos; it took decades, if not centuries, and the reigns of several competent kings for Egypt to finally recover and usher in another golden age. After ruling the lands for slightly over fifty years, Mentuhotep II left the world of the living to take his seat among the gods, leaving his throne and legacy to his son, Sankhkare Mentuhotep III.

Believed to have taken the mantle at an old age, Mentuhotep III ruled over Egypt for only twelve years. Despite his short reign, he managed to permanently carve his name into the history books, mostly because of his success in his expedition to Punt—an expedition that had not been undertaken since the last rulers of the Old Kingdom. As Mentuhotep III stepped into the eighth year of his reign, the king sent at least three thousand men under the command of his most trusted steward, known as Henenu, toward the Red Sea, where they were tasked with ridding the region of any rebels and reopening the trade routes to Punt and Libya. The expedition's success rewarded Egypt with precious resources, as the troops returned to Gebtu with incense, perfumes, gum, and stones quarried from Wadi Hammamat, a major mining and quarrying region near the Nile.

Apart from expeditions, Mentuhotep III was also praised for his construction projects. The Temple of Montu, which was thought to have been built by the rulers of the Old Kingdom to honor the falcon-headed god of war, was further extended under Mentuhotep III's orders. Parts of the structure that feature a relief of the king still survive to this day and are currently on display in the Louvre.

Another temple dedicated to Montu was erected on top of Thoth Hill, the highest peak overlooking Egypt's Valley of the Kings. This mud-brick temple was destroyed, possibly due to a terrible earthquake that terrorized the land at the end of the Eleventh Dynasty. Perhaps to honor and thank his father for bestowing a nearly prosperous kingdom upon him, the king finished many of Mentuhotep II's unfinished projects at Abydos, Elkab, Armant, El-Tod, and Elephantine.

The remnants of the Temple of Montu.
https://commons.wikimedia.org/wiki/File:Medmoud_vue_g%C3%A9n%C3%A9rale.JPG

Mentuhotep III died sometime around 1998 BCE—some sources claim he died earlier—and what happened after his death was not properly documented, leading to several views. The Turin Royal Canon, an ancient papyrus that contains a list of Egypt's kings, claims that after Mentuhotep III passed, the Egyptians lived without a ruler for seven years. However, with what little evidence that was left and discovered, Egyptologists have come to the conclusion that Egypt welcomed another king, though his reign was not as great as his predecessor's.

The throne was said to have been passed to Mentuhotep III's son, who went by the name of Mentuhotep IV. His reign was even shorter than his father's; the last king of the Eleventh Dynasty ruled over Egypt for only six years. No inscriptions about his deeds survived. However, it is plausible that Mentuhotep IV was way past his glory days when he took the reins and had already predicted his demise. During his early years on the throne, the king was believed to have put his entire focus on building a perfect tomb for himself. He entrusted his vizier, Amenemhat, with an important mission. The old king ordered him to travel outside the safe walls of Thebes to search for high-quality stones that could be used to craft an intricate royal sarcophagus. Amenemhat discovered a quarry during his travels, thus completing his mission. The site exists today and features an inscription that credited Amenemhat's effort in realizing his king's wish.

When Mentuhotep IV finally died due to an unknown reason, Egypt was yet again troubled since he left neither a successor nor an heir. Amenemhat, who likely saw an opportunity to expand his power, took the mantle and claimed himself to be the new king of Egypt and the founder of the Twelfth Dynasty. How he rose to the throne remains a mystery. Some suggest that he did so peacefully, while others claim that he was the one who had secretly murdered Mentuhotep IV. We do know that his reign was not widely accepted at the beginning.

A relief depicting Amenemhat I.
Metropolitan Museum of Art, CC0, via Wikimedia Commons:
https://commons.wikimedia.org/wiki/File:Lintel_of_Amenemhat_I_and_Deities_MET_D P322055.jpg

Now referred to as Amenemhat I, the new king made a move to further strengthen his position. The king knew he had created many enemies, especially since he did not have royal blood flowing through his veins. Early on, Amenemhat was forced to face at least two rivals who also claimed the Egyptian throne. However, Amenemhat successfully removed the threat without heavy resistance. After obtaining some support from his people, who were beginning to accept him as their new ruler, Amenemhat filled his early days on the throne with sailing up and down the Nile to vanquish the rebels and those who exposed even the slightest signs of opposition.

He was indeed unpopular during the early years of his reign. He initially ruled with an iron fist, which further pushed the Egyptians away from him. One nomarch who went by the name Nehri specifically claimed that Amenemhat was so ruthless that he had to rescue his town from the king's terror. In contrast, those who willingly and faithfully bowed to the new pharaoh were greatly rewarded and saved from punishment. Many of them were even made the new nomarchs and viziers.

Eventually, Amenemhat I successfully quenched the rebellions and restored order across the kingdom. To prove to his people that his reign was nothing but the start of a new golden era, the Egyptian king commenced several construction projects, with most of them dedicated to the mightiest god, Amun. Although what remains of Amenemhat's biggest temple are only pieces, the temple was absorbed into a complex built by the rulers of the New Kingdom a few hundred years later. Today, the remnants of Amenemhat's temple can be found in the massive Karnak Temple Complex.

Thirty years into Amenemhat's reign over the vast land of the Nile, he began the construction of Amenemhat-itj-tawy (more commonly known as Itjtawy), which soon became the capital city of the Twelfth Dynasty. From the king's point of view, the city was important since it acted as a symbol of the Egyptian civilization's rebirth. Through this rebirth, Amenemhat was able to revive old traditions. The pyramid, which had last been built over two centuries before Amenemhat's reign, began to make a comeback. The king even went as far as to reuse the blocks from the Great Pyramid to construct his own pyramid, hoping it could match or perhaps surpass the standards set during the Old Kingdom.

Aside from reviving the old traditions and ordering massive construction projects, the king was also credited with restoring and strengthening Egypt's influence abroad. Ever since the chaotic rule of the Sixth Dynasty, Egypt's borders gradually waned, which led to the arrival of raiders from each corner of the kingdom's borders. The east was terrorized by the Canaanites, while the Libyans showed their fangs in the west and the Nubians in the south. Upon witnessing the uprising of the Nubians, who established their own state and gave themselves royal titles that imitated the Egyptian kings (one of them claimed to be the living son of Ra), Amenemhat launched a strategy to suppress the Nubians and secure the Egyptian borders. He first built fortresses along the frontier. During the last ten years of his reign, the king launched a full attack against Lower Nubia. The Nubian town of Buhen, which was strategically located near the Nile's Second Cataract, was captured by the Egyptians and converted into one of Egypt's greatest fortresses. With that, Egypt managed to reestablish its military influence in Nubia, thus paving the way for the kingdom to reopen and extend its trade routes.

To secure his legacy and ensure Egypt's prosperity, Amenemhat was careful not to leave the throne without a successor. Sometime during his twentieth year of rule, the king named his son, Senusret, as his successor. To show his son the ropes, Amenemhat appointed him as co-regent.

When the news of his father's sudden death reached Senusret, he did not hesitate to claim his rights to the throne. Legend has it that he was visited by his deceased father in his dreams. His dead father later explained the reason behind his death: he had been assassinated by his own bodyguards. Advised by his father not to put his complete trust in anyone, Senusret tracked down every possible rival and quickly eliminated them. His relentless advance soon reached beyond the borders of Egypt, as he successfully launched campaigns against Nubia all the way to the Third Cataract of the Nile, which rewarded Egypt with attractive supplies of gold and copper.

With the new riches he obtained after pacifying the south, Senusret followed in his father's footsteps, filling the lands with even more impressive structures. One of his most popular constructions that still stands today is the obelisk in Heliopolis, which measures at least twenty meters (sixty-five feet) in height.

The obelisk of Senusret.
https://commons.wikimedia.org/wiki/File:Heliopolis200501.JPG

Senusret ruled over Egypt for forty-five years and was succeeded by his son, Amenemhat II, who went down in Egyptian history as yet another one of the Middle Kingdom's most powerful rulers, mostly because of his successful military campaigns and trade policies. Following the tradition started by Amenemhat I, the king appointed his son, Senusret II, as co-regent and passed the mantle to him when he finally died after thirty-five years of ruling. Although Senusret II's reign was described as a period of peace, thanks to the continuous efforts of his predecessors, Senusret III has been branded as the most remembered king of the Twelfth Dynasty.

As Egypt continued to prosper, the kingdom witnessed rapid growth in its population. However, this growth troubled Senusret III since the central government began to show signs of weakening, especially when the nomarchs started to rule their respective provinces more independently. To prevent history from repeating itself and to remove any possibility of yet another civil war, Senusret III introduced a new political reform. Under the reform, the nomarchs were called back to the capital and given positions in court, thus cutting them off from overseeing the operations within their territories. By moving the nomarchs to the capital, Senusret could keep a close eye on them and easily put a stop to their plans should they show signs of opposition.

Apart from stabilizing the central government, Senusret was also credited with protecting Egyptian borders and trade routes. In the early years of his reign, the king launched a series of devastating campaigns against Nubia and emerged victorious most of the time to the point where the king was able to boast his success on a great stele erected in Semna. Senusret III claimed that, under his leadership, the campaigns led to many Nubian deaths, while women were taken as slaves, their crops destroyed, and their water sources poisoned. New fortresses were built along the frontier, which greatly helped his future campaigns.

However, Nubia was not the only region that the king paid attention to, as he also led his troops against Syria. While Senusret III aimed to expand his power, the campaign in Syria was also done to secure precious resources. Most of the plunder was directed toward the great temples in Egypt. The pharaoh ordered the reconstruction of the temples and refurbished them with loads of valuable stones, such as lapis lazuli, gold, and malachite.

Senusret III was succeeded by his son, Amenemhat III, who had served the kingdom during his father's reign as co-regent. Amenemhat resumed his father's projects. Sometime during his forty-five years on the throne, Egypt reached its peak, which was mostly owed to the king's efforts to elevate the kingdom's economic state. His work on the water system greatly benefited Egypt's farming activities, and his involvement in upgrading the facilities near the turquoise mines in Sinai was also appreciated by many.

Aside from commissioning a temple for the goddess of love and fertility, Hathor, Amenemhat III's greatest achievement in architecture was the Labyrinth, an impressive, long-lost underground complex that was described by the Greek historian Herodotus.

Chapter 7: Decline of the Middle Kingdom and the Reign of the Hyksos during the Second Intermediate Period

After the death of Sobekneferu, Egyptologists are again left with only mysteries and questions since little evidence survived that could describe the events that took place in the kingdom. The Turin Royal Canon mentions a few kings who ruled over the lands after the end of the Twelfth Dynasty, but the record is damaged and far from complete. The Thirteenth Dynasty has been described by historians as rather obscure. No one has been able to determine how the first king of the Thirteenth Dynasty took over the mantle from Sobekneferu, the first female pharaoh, though most sources agree there was no bloodbath involved; instead, the throne passed to the next ruler peacefully. It is plausible that Sobekneferu, like her predecessor, did not name anyone to succeed her. Without a child of her own or even an heir from her immediate family, Egypt was left with no choice but to welcome a new ruler from a completely different family.

The identity of the first king of the Thirteenth Dynasty remains a mystery. The chronology of this period is often described by Egyptologists as confusing. Nevertheless, the unnamed king faced little to zero obstacles when he claimed the throne, as there were no signs of threats or rebellions. However, this did not mean that Egypt was going through a period of peace, as many sources claim the kingdom witnessed nearly 70 different kings in the course of 150 years. Like the First Intermediate Period, these short reigns of dozens of kings were a huge sign of political instability. This was a new era of Egypt known to history as the Second Intermediate Period.

Fortunately, the kingdom never went through major changes during the first few decades of the Thirteenth Dynasty. The rulers still even reigned from the same capital, Itjtawy, possibly due to the systematic government bureaucracy established by the great rulers of the previous dynasty. The kingdom was overseen by not only the king but also his viziers, other high officials, and civil servants. Egyptologists have even suggested that the king was merely a figurehead during this period of time. He might have only played an important role for religious reasons.

But, of course, without a highly capable ruler at the helm, the power of the central government waned. Unlike the great kings of the late Twelfth Dynasty, the rulers of the Thirteenth Dynasty barely left their throne in the capital of Itjtawy. Without the ruler's oversight, the provinces began to drift apart, and the central government gradually lost its effectiveness. During Sobekhotep IV's reign, Egypt began to see clearer signs of a collapse. Although historians and scholars agree that he was the most powerful ruler of the dynasty, the kingdom's future had been written and could not be altered. The many fortresses built along the frontiers in the south were beginning to be abandoned, with many of the guards and soldiers stationed at the garrisons choosing to defect and side with the growing power of the Nubian Kingdom of Kush. Almost the same could be said about the fortresses in Sinai and Canaan. Since there were fewer troops in the garrisons, the men were eventually disbanded or called back to the capital.

Trouble was also brewing on the eastern branch of the Nile Delta, particularly in the city of Avaris. Initially founded by Amenemhat I of the Twelfth Dynasty, the city was mostly inhabited by immigrants who typically originated from western Asia and parts of the Levant. Some of these immigrants were sent to Egypt as slaves, although there were also those who willingly came in search of work that could reward them with enough food on the table. They could work at one of the many construction sites scattered throughout the valley.

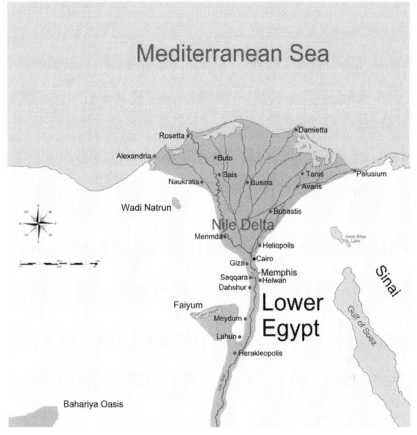

The city of Avaris in Lower Egypt.

Ancient_Egypt_map-en.svg: Jeff Dahlderivative work: MinisterForBadTimes, CC BY-SA 3.0 <https://creativecommons.org/licenses/by-sa/3.0>, via Wikimedia Commons: https://commons.wikimedia.org/wiki/File:Lower_Egypt-en.png

Since Avaris was strategically located near the shores of the Mediterranean Sea, the city became a popular spot for traders, which eventually attracted even more immigrants, especially Canaanites. Despite retaining most of their culture, the Canaanites who called Avaris their new home were culturally Egyptianized over time. Around 1800 BCE, when the Middle Kingdom was at its peak, these Egyptianized Canaanites began to populate big cities across the kingdom. Some of those who remained in Avaris managed to secure positions within the Egyptian government, while many others grew extremely wealthy from their flourishing trade businesses.

Upon witnessing the weakening of the central government, especially when the king's power was barely present in the many provinces, these wealthy immigrants began to devise a plan of their own to further assert their power and influence in the vast kingdom. Sometime between 1750 BCE and 1700 BCE, a new dynasty was born. The Fourteenth Dynasty was mostly made up of rulers from Canaan and the Levant. The dynasty is considered even more of a mystery than the Thirteenth Dynasty. However, we do know that the rulers of this newly formed dynasty reigned from the city of Avaris. The two dynasties coexisted with each other and were believed to have had a difficult time expanding their power. The Egyptians were again faced with a famine, and both dynasties struggled to make ends meet due to the terrible economic state caused by the worsening trade businesses.

Despite having the support of the majority of the provinces in Upper Egypt, the Thirteenth Dynasty was unable to make a move and secure the territories in the Eastern Delta, which was controlled by the ruler of the Fourteenth Dynasty. The latter was also incapable of expanding his influence beyond the Nile Delta due to his state's weak military. This inadvertently opened the door for a stronger group of people to showcase their power and invade the kingdom. They came from the east and were referred to in the Egyptian tongue as *heka khasut*, more commonly known to us as the Hyksos ("rulers of foreign lands").

This was the first time Egypt was forced to bow down to a foreign power. However, how the Hyksos breached the kingdom and asserted their dominance over the vast valley remains a debate. According to Manetho, they were believed to have entered Egypt on chariots from the east while carrying compound bows and other advanced technology of the Bronze Age. Also referred to as invaders, the Hyksos took over Lower Egypt with force. Oppression was their absolute answer to ensure the Egyptians gave in. Manetho claimed that they not only sacked the rulers of the land with great aggression but also burned several Egyptian cities, destroying many of the kingdom's most sacred temples. The Egyptians who survived the brutal massacre and surrendered were far from safe. They were subjected to slavery; even women and children were not spared.

With the Egyptians—be it the nobles or the commoners—either lying lifeless on the ground or forced into slavery, the Hyksos appointed one of their own to be Egypt's new king. The king was known as Salitis, and he ruled from Memphis with an iron fist. He was succeeded by five more kings, whose combined reigns lasted for at least a century. However, Manetho's record about the Hyksos is to be taken with a grain of salt, especially since his descriptions of the event were written at least 1,400 years after the invasion and were infused with biased opinions. While Manetho claimed the Hyksos used violence to conquer the northern part of Egypt, archaeological findings suggest otherwise. Since there were no clear signs of heavy casualties and damage in most of the major cities of the Eastern Delta, including Avaris, Egyptologists arrived at the conclusion that the invasion was not a terror campaign as Manetho suggested.

Nonetheless, the Hyksos rulers had successfully expanded their influence by 1600 BCE. From initially sowing their seeds of power only in the cities scattered throughout the Eastern Delta, the invaders extended their rule as far as the region of Beni Hasan in Middle Egypt. However, while the Hyksos were occupied with expanding their grasp over half of the kingdom, another dynasty was born, this time in Thebes. Classified as the Sixteenth Dynasty, some sources claim that it was, in fact, established by what was left of the obscure Thirteenth Dynasty, whose members could have possibly sought refuge in Thebes. Others suggest that it was a completely new line of rulers founded by a Theban family. Whatever its origins might be, we can be sure that the rulers of the Sixteenth Dynasty constantly faced conflicts and obstacles. Thebes was located in the middle of the chaos; the northern regions were mostly conquered by the Hyksos, while the Egyptian fortresses in the south were under the control of the Kushites. Raids from the Hyksos, rebellions from the natives, and famine shook the dynasty and its capital.

The Hyksos and their many regions, on the other hand, were blooming. The population was steadily growing, and the economy flourished. The Hyksos rulers managed to elevate Egypt's trade links with almost all parts of the known world. Various objects from the Levant began to emerge more often than before in the local markets, attracting even more traders. The Hyksos kings were also believed to have made contact with rulers from other kingdoms. For instance, one particular king known as Khyan had his name carved on a few artifacts that were possibly sent to different kingdoms of the ancient world. A set of bowls with an inscription of the king's name was once discovered in Hattusa, an ancient city in central Turkey, and a few other objects bearing the king's name were also found in Knossos, the capital of the Minoan civilization.

The regions under the Hyksos witnessed an increasing number of new temples, although most of them were constructed in honor of the Canaanite god of fertility, Baal, rather than the Egyptian deities. Of course, with their stability and growing power, the Hyksos rulers, specifically Apepi and Khamudi, began to work on an even bigger ambition. They planned to have all of Egypt within their grasp and remove any rivals that stood in the way.

Under King Seqenenre Tao of the Seventeenth Dynasty, Egypt finally began to oppose the Hyksos. According to Manetho, the Egyptian king was said to have been insulted by the Hyksos king, Apepi, which eventually resulted in a vicious battle. Not planning to let a foreign invader tarnish his reputation, Seqenenre Tao gathered his troops and marched out of Thebes. However, luck was not on Seqenenre's side, as the fight was won by the Hyksos. It could be plausible that Seqenenre fell in one of the skirmishes against the Hyksos since his mummy was discovered with battle wounds.

The Thebans were then led by another king of the Seventeenth Dynasty, Kamose, who was the son of Seqenenre. The Theban king had enough of the taxes imposed by the Hyksos government. He resumed his father's campaign and tried to realize his dream, which was to free the lands of Egypt from a foreign power. After spending most of his time on the throne strategizing, Kamose launched a devastating attack on Avaris and slaughtered those who stood in his way or showed support for the Hyksos. Although his inscription tells us that he successfully ravaged the fortified city of Avaris to the ground, Egyptologists agree the description of the event might include a touch of exaggeration. The Hyksos still controlled Lower

Egypt after the attacks launched by Kamose.

After leading the Thebans for possibly three to five years, Kamose was succeeded by his brother, who went by the name Ahmose. Taking the mantle when he was only a child, Ahmose, like his predecessors, had the same ambition: to drive the foreign rulers out of Egypt once and for all. He spearheaded several campaigns against the last Hyksos king, Khamudi. Kamose launched multiple attacks and quelled a few rebellions that were brewing in the south. The Theban king then reconquered parts of Lower Egypt.

Sources claim that it took four attacks against Avaris before Ahmose could finally capture the fortified city. After the Hyksos were finally defeated, they retreated out of Egypt and took shelter in the town of Sharuhen, which was turned into their next stronghold. However, the Theban king was far from done with the foreign invaders, as he went on to showcase his military prowess by besieging the stronghold. After years of laying siege to Sharuhen, the Hyksos fell, thus freeing Egypt from the hands of foreign rulers. With the fall of the Hyksos, Egypt was set in motion to enter another booming era: the New Kingdom.

Chapter 8: The New Kingdom: Egypt's Most Glorious Era

If it was not for Ahmose I, Egypt might have suffered even longer under the reign of the ruthless Hyksos kings. Ahmose claimed the throne when he was barely an adult—sources claim that he was ten at the time. He did not only avenge the death of his father and free Egypt from foreign invaders, but he also founded the Eighteenth Dynasty. Although his success in driving out the Hyksos was admired and cheered for by nearly all of his subjects, Ahmose was not planning to slow down, especially since the kingdom was in dire need of restoration.

After moving the capital to Thebes, the king shifted his entire focus to the power-hungry Nubians. During his reign, Egypt was able to reassert its control over the south, specifically the Nubian territories. Their gold supplies were plundered and transferred to the Egyptian treasury. Seeing how his kingdom was still far from achieving economic stability, Ahmose reopened mines, quarries, and trade routes throughout Egypt. Many construction projects also started to take place under his rule. The temples and monuments that had been destroyed by the invaders were restored or rebuilt, and many other structures built by the Hyksos kings were destroyed in an effort to bury all traces of their power. After laying the foundations for Egypt's New Kingdom, Ahmose died after at least twenty-five years on the throne. His success was remembered by his subjects to the point where he was worshiped as a god as soon as news of his passing reached the public.

Hatshepsut, the Once Forgotten Female Pharaoh of Egypt

The act of removing evidence and contributions of prior rulers from the official accounts—later known by the Romans as *damnatio memoriae*—was not only applied to the Hyksos. Believe it or not, Hatshepsut was one of the many rulers who were subjected to the act. Her statues were destroyed, her public recognition was erased from official documents, and her contributions to many impressive constructions were never mentioned by later pharaohs and scribes. However, the reason behind the condemnation of her memory remains disputed. Some suggest the main reason was that the Egyptians were not fully accepting of a female taking the mantle of pharaoh. Others claim that her traces of power were actually erased by Thutmose III, her stepson, who possibly held a grudge toward her for taking the throne away from him.

Hatshepsut was first appointed as regent to the young Thutmose III before she claimed her spot as a fully-fledged pharaoh. Although her reign was successful, it caused many of her subjects to be dissatisfied, possibly because of her gender. Although women in ancient Egypt had almost the same rights as men (women in ancient Egypt could start their own businesses, own properties, marry and divorce their partners, and even become witnesses in court), allowing a female to be crowned as the ruler might have been a tad too much. The Egyptians believed that by placing Hatshepsut at the top of their hierarchy, they could cause a disturbance to Ma'at, the balance of the world. Having her as a ruler disrupted their centuries-long tradition of male rulers. It also contradicted their belief that a pharaoh was supposed to be the living embodiment of Horus, the male god of war.

It could be plausible that Hatshepsut was well aware of the issues that would arise if she continued to ignore her subjects' dissatisfaction. In the seventh year of her reign, she began to make some changes, especially in terms of how her reliefs and statues depicted her. She was often pictured as a male pharaoh and sometimes referred to herself as Hatshepsu, which contained a masculine ending. However, this did not completely solve her problems since her image was almost entirely erased from the kingdom following her death.

The Sphinx of Hatshepsut.
Sphinx_of_Hatshepsut.jpg: Postdlf/derivative work: JMCC1, CC BY-SA 3.0
<http://creativecommons.org/licenses/by-sa/3.0/>, via Wikimedia Commons:
https://commons.wikimedia.org/wiki/File:Sphinx_of_Hatshepsut_c.jpg

Even though she was once removed from history, Egyptologists today recognize her as one of the most notable pharaohs to rule over Egypt during the New Kingdom. Regarded as a great builder,

Hatshepsut commissioned various construction projects across the kingdom. Her mortuary temple, Djeser-Djeseru, is considered one of the most impressive architectural achievements of the ancient world and is still standing today. Egypt also owed parts of its booming economy to the female pharaoh since she was the one who commandeered the successful and lavish expedition to the land of Punt, Egypt's trade partner since the Middle Kingdom. Her military campaigns mostly centered around the regions of Nubia and Syria. Her inscriptions claim that she marched alongside her army in battle. To put it simply, Hatshepsut was a capable ruler, just like some of the other male rulers of Egypt. Most of her traces might have been removed, but the remaining fragments of her reign that survived were enough to attest to her deeds.

Thutmose III and the Battle of Megiddo

It is believed that Thutmose III spent most of his youth proving he could be one of Egypt's most powerful pharaohs. He participated in a number of campaigns launched by his stepmother, Hatshepsut, giving him a chance to sharpen his military skills. He was even appointed as the head of the army by Hatshepsut the moment he reached adulthood. So, when his ruling stepmother passed away sometime in 1458 BCE, Thutmose immediately assumed the title of the sixth pharaoh of the Eighteenth Dynasty.

Although he had been left with a prosperous kingdom and well-trained military, the new pharaoh was not able to enjoy a minute of peace since he was forced to face threats imposed by the leaders of the Levant, who thought he was a weak leader. The rebels threatened to turn their backs on the kingdom or, worse, invade Egypt if he refused to step down. Being a great military strategist, Thutmose refused to bargain with the rebels and launched an attack on the ancient city of Megiddo (better known by its Greek name, Armageddon). Leading his troops at the front, Thutmose laid siege to the city. After seven to eight months, the rebels were left with no choice but to surrender, as they faced starvation.

Despite gaining a victory, Thutmose did not cause any further bloodshed within the city. Instead, he offered a deal. In return for leaving the city and the rebels almost unscathed, Thutmose demanded they sheathe their weapons and ensure there would be no more rebellions in the future, to which they agreed. However, he did strip the rebels of their positions and powers before appointing new officials who had been loyal to him. Children of the rebellion's leaders were taken as hostages and brought back to Egypt. They were treated with kindness and granted an Egyptian education. They were only allowed to return to their homeland once they came of age.

A relief at Karnak depicting Thutmose III slaying his enemy at the battle of Megiddo.
Olaf Tausch, CC BY 3.0 <https://creativecommons.org/licenses/by/3.0>, via Wikimedia Commons: https://commons.wikimedia.org/wiki/File:Karnak_Tempel_15.jpg

The success of this particular campaign no doubt increased Egypt's standing in the Near East. From this battle alone, Thutmose and his fierce military obtained lucrative spoils of war. The Battle of Megiddo was the first battle in history recorded in detail. The troops brought back 340 captives, over 20,000 sheep, 2,238 horses, nearly 1,000 cattle and chariots, 552 bows, and 200 fine pieces of armor. With this victory, Egypt easily asserted its dominance over northern Canaan. Thutmose's military achievement was celebrated not only by his loyal subjects but also by the kingdom's neighboring empires. Kings from Babylon, Assyria, and Anatolia were among the leaders who sent tributary gifts to the pharaoh following his victory.

However, Thutmose III's campaigns did not stop there. The great pharaoh soon commenced more successful campaigns to Nubia, the Kingdom of Mitanni, parts of Phoenicia, and Kadesh. With his long list of military triumphs, Thutmose III went down in history as the deadliest Egyptian pharaoh who greatly expanded the kingdom's borders.

Akhenaten, the Heretic Pharaoh

Akhenaten rose to the throne at least a century after Thutmose III. He gained a kingdom that was already at its peak largely due to previous pharaohs' successful attempts at expanding Egypt's borders. By the time he was crowned, his vast kingdom had its fingers firmly wrapped around the neighboring regions, including Palestine, Nubia, and Phoenicia.

However, Akhenaten was known by a different name when he first claimed the mantle; he was known to his subject as Amenhotep IV. It was only during his fifth year on the throne that the pharaoh changed his name to Akhenaten. The reason behind this was largely due to his decision to introduce a new religion to the kingdom. Although Akhenaten was first said to have worshiped the traditional gods of Egypt, such as Amun, Ra, and Osiris, the pharaoh chose to abandon the old gods and establish a monotheistic religion. Why exactly Akhenaten decided to defy the traditional beliefs of the ancient Egyptians remains a question, but certain sources suggested that part of it was due to the influences brought into the kingdom by foreigners settling in the land of the Nile.

Known as Atenism or the Amarna heresy, the religion centered around the sun god Aten. No clear details remain today that can tell us more about the new religion; however, we do know that, unlike the old gods, Aten was depicted in neither his animal nor human form. In fact, the new god was often represented by only a sun disk with several lines of sun ways extending downward. Since the monotheistic religion forced the Egyptians to worship only Aten, Atenism was not widely accepted by many, especially those who were not willing to neglect their centuries-old king of gods, Amun.

And so, Akhenaten resorted to closing down all of the temples that were once dedicated to the old gods—a move that forever harmed his reputation. Even the name of the great god of the afterlife, Osiris, was erased, as the Egyptians were forced to seek blessings for the dead from the one and only Aten. The capital was also moved from Thebes to a newly constructed city called Akhetaten ("Horizon of the Aten"), which is now known as Amarna.

Apart from his infamous religious reforms, the pharaoh also lost the support of his subjects when he paid little to zero interest in performing his kingship responsibilities; he paid no attention to the military and neglected the kingdom's trade and economy. Since the pharaoh chose to focus more on the newly founded religion rather than running the kingdom, local officials began to take advantage of the situation. Most of the taxes collected from the people of Egypt went directly into their pockets.

During his last years on the throne, the pharaoh was left with no choice but to deal with many of his discontent subjects, especially the army commanders and priests. It was also believed that the pharaoh even became estranged from his wife and strongest supporter, Nefertiti, during his last years. He finally died seventeen years after his rise to the throne. A few years after his burial, the pharaoh's sarcophagus was destroyed, and his city was completely abandoned—Akhenaten was indeed hated even after death. He was then succeeded by an obscure figure known by the name of Smenkhkare.

While some were certain that Smenkhkare was Akhenaten's co-regent and assumed to be his nephew, brother, or son, other sources suggest that Smenkhkare was none other than the heretic pharaoh's own wife, Nefertiti. Due to the troubles Hatshepsut faced, it would not be a surprise if Nefertiti chose to rule the kingdom under a male alias. If this, by any chance, is true, we could be sure that Nefertiti was the one who was responsible for the beginning of the kingdom's religious change. After the death of Akhenaten, the Egyptians slowly reverted to their ancient beliefs and traditions. The worship of the sun god Aten was nowhere to be seen, while the temples of Amun and the other old gods began to reappear. However, the reign of Smenkhkare (or Nefertiti) only lasted for a short while, but the next pharaoh, Tutankhamun (the son of Akhenaten), would continue to reverse his father's religious changes and erase his footsteps. It was only when the young pharaoh rose to the throne that ancient Egypt was able to fully return to its polytheistic roots.

Ramesses II and the Battle of Kadesh

The Eighteenth Dynasty ended with the death of Pharaoh Horemheb, who had no heir to succeed him. However, despite having no surviving son who could continue his legacy, Horemheb had one particular individual in mind to whom he would pass the throne. His name was Paramesse, and he once served the pharaoh as his chief vizier. The main reason behind Horemheb's decision to appoint Paramesse as his successor is uncertain. Some claim that the pharaoh completely trusted his vizier since he had long portrayed his undying loyalty to the Egyptian royals, while there are others who claim that it was possibly because Paramesse had both a son and a grandson, thus saving the kingdom from any future power struggles.

With the death of Horemheb in 1292 BCE, Paramesse rose to the throne, just as the late pharaoh had wished. He adopted the name Ramesses I and founded the Nineteenth Dynasty, which comprised some of Egypt's most successful rulers. The second king of the dynasty, Seti I, soon led Egypt to become the power center of the ancient world. His successful reign saw the expansion of the kingdom, as the pharaoh was able to reclaim the territories once lost during the reign of the heretic pharaoh Akhenaten. To prepare his son for the throne, Seti I appointed fourteen-year-old Ramesses II as prince regent. The pharaoh also introduced his son to the military by bringing him on his many campaigns. After obtaining enough skills, the teenage Ramesses was appointed as the captain of the Egyptian troops.

After eleven years on the throne, Seti I moved on from the world of the living and made his journey to the underworld, leaving his son, whom he had well prepared for the throne, to rise as the new pharaoh of Egypt. Ramesses II (later known as Ramesses the Great) no doubt possessed an extensive experience of the battlefield due to his involvement in Seti I's many campaigns. One of his two greatest military achievements happened during his second year on the throne. At the time, Egypt was continuously threatened by the Sea Peoples, who were described by the Egyptians as pirates possibly originating from Ionia. They were called the Sherden. After receiving reports of pirates terrorizing the local populations and pillaging a great number of Egyptian vessels along the Mediterranean coast, the pharaoh ordered a retaliation.

A colossal statue of Ramesses II at Memphis.
Dominik Knippel, de:Niedernberg, CC BY-SA 3.0
<http://creativecommons.org/licenses/by-sa/3.0/>, via Wikimedia Commons:
https://commons.wikimedia.org/wiki/File:Kolosstatue_Ramses_II_Memphis.jpg

Ramesses knew going against the pirates head-on would only cause higher casualties. So, the pharaoh strategized a trap to lure the pirates into an ambush. A number of cargo-laden vessels were positioned in a specific area off the coast to act as bait. The Sherden, who took the bait, were immediately surrounded by a fleet of Egyptian warships. Within a short time, the Egyptians, led by the cunning pharaoh, successfully defeated the pirates, resulting in their capture. Those who survived the ambush were brought to the capital city of Pi-Ramesses (modern-day Qantir) and forced to serve the pharaoh as his personal bodyguards until their last breath. These bodyguards, who were often depicted wearing horned helmets and equipped with round shields and huge swords, were said to have accompanied the pharaoh in many of his battles.

A relief of Ramesses II capturing his enemies from Nubia, Libya, and Syria.
Speedster, CC BY-SA 4.0 <https://creativecommons.org/licenses/by-sa/4.0>, via Wikimedia Commons: https://commons.wikimedia.org/wiki/File:Ramses-ii-relief-from-memphis2.png

Ramesses II's most remarkable military achievement was none other than his battle with the Hittites. Known as the Battle of Kadesh, the conflict took place in 1274 BCE near an important trade city in Syria called Kadesh. The tension between the Egyptians and the Hittites had long existed; the Hittites were believed to have caused trouble in the valley, especially during the reign of Thutmose III. Ramesses II's father, Seti I, successfully captured Kadesh but not for long, as the Hittites were able to reclaim and fortify the city to ensure they could withstand any future invasion by the Egyptians. Sources claim that the strain between the two escalated when Ramesses launched his campaigns into Canaan, during which a Hittite vassal was captured. Upon hearing of the capture, the Hittite king, Muwatalli II, decided to confront the Egyptian pharaoh in battle.

Ramesses II, who was eager to capture Kadesh and benefit from its booming trade and location, gathered the Egyptian forces, which counted at least twenty thousand infantry and two thousand chariots, in preparation for the upcoming war. He then organized them into four divisions named after the Egyptian gods: Amun, Ra, Ptah, and Set. The king of the Hittites raised a greater force of almost forty thousand infantry and three thousand chariots. The Egyptian pharaoh might have been popular for his military brilliance, but many forgot that he, too, was a human being. Ramesses II was thought to have made his first mistake by marching with the Amun division too fast, thus leaving the rest far behind.

After moving through the Gaza Strip, he set up camp about eleven kilometers away from Kadesh. The pharaoh and his forces stumbled upon a couple of tribal nomads, who informed the Egyptian king of Muwatalli's location: he was said to be camping in the land of Aleppo, some two hundred kilometers away from Kadesh. This, however, turned out to be false information; the nomads were actually hired by the Hittites to purposely confuse the Egyptians. Ramesses II was afterward presented with two Hittite prisoners who were brought back by one of his scouts. The captives were tortured and finally revealed the real location of the Hittite king. Muwatalli and his troops were camped right on the other side of Kadesh.

Ramesses II in his chariot attacking the Hittites.
https://commons.wikimedia.org/wiki/File:Ramses_II_besieging_the_Cheta_people_in_Dapur.jpg

Muwatalli II and his troops hastily charged toward the Ra division, which had been left behind by the Amun division. The Hittites then moved on to round up Ramesses and his Amun division, causing havoc. The pharaoh himself claimed that his forces panicked and scrambled from the battlefield, leaving him to deal with the enemies alone. Whether or not his claim was true, we do know that the pharaoh, along with the remaining charioteers and infantrymen of the Amun division, launched a counterattack against the Hittites. After regrouping, Muwatalli II planned another attack against Ramesses, but his plan was cut short upon the Ptah division's arrival from the south.

The battle resumed the following day. The Hittites were forced to retreat, allowing Ramesses II to advance on the city of Kadesh. However, the Egyptians were unable to recapture the city, possibly due to their inability to lay a long siege on a fully fortified city. Having no other choice, Ramesses II led his troops back to Egypt. The Battle of Kadesh was a stalemate, but the conflicts between the two sides continued for years to come. Due to the rising Assyrian threat to the east, the new Hittite king, Hattusili III, decided to halt any further attacks against Egypt. About fifteen years after the great battle, a peace treaty was signed by Ramesses II and Hattusili III. With the Egyptian-Hittite peace treaty, sometimes known as the Treaty of Kadesh (the earliest surviving peace treaty), Egypt and the Hittite Empire put down their weapons and ended their centuries of bloodshed.

Chapter 9: The Third Intermediate Period: The Kushite Empire

The ancient Egyptians, like the other ancient civilizations, believed in polytheism. Ra, Osiris, Horus, Set, Ptah, Anubis, and Hathor are some of the most popular deities often worshiped by the Egyptians. The gods were believed to be the creators and sustainers of all life, so honoring and pleasing them would be one of the few ways to ensure blessings in one's life, be it in the form of health, wealth, or even peace.

However, by the start of the New Kingdom, another god came to prominence. This particular god went from being a local deity during the Old Kingdom to the patron god of the pharaohs centuries later. He was referred to as Amun, whose name can be translated as the "Hidden One" due to its association with the wind. First gaining popularity in Thebes, Amun was believed to be the god who created all things, including himself.

The ancient Egyptian god of Amun.

Jeff Dahl, CC BY-SA 4.0 <https://creativecommons.org/licenses/by-sa/4.0>, via Wikimedia Commons: https://commons.wikimedia.org/wiki/File:Amun.svg

In the beginning, the god was worshiped alongside the falcon-headed Ra as two different divine entities. It was only sometime around the 16th century BCE that the two powerful gods were fused together to become Amun-Ra, the chief of the Egyptian pantheon. For centuries, Amun's influence greatly expanded, with his high priests typically placed at the top of the hierarchy, second only to the kings since pharaohs were considered Egypt's "First Priest." The high priests of Amun were thought to have been blessed with a special relation to the god and were expected to tend to his needs. If a certain unfortunate event took place in the Nile Valley, such as famine, plague, and even poverty, the priests were responsible for finding out the reason behind the god's wrath and looking for ways to mend the problem.

Over time, the priests of Amun gained so much influence and power over the land that they owned even more land compared to the pharaoh. Their prominence waned during the reign of Akhenaten, the pharaoh who worshiped the sun god Aten and attempted to convert Egypt into a monotheistic kingdom. However, the priests managed to regain their influence after the pharaoh's death and were at their height during the reign of Ramesses XI, the last king of the Twentieth Dynasty.

The Division of Power in Egypt

Egypt was again heading toward chaos and instability under Ramesses XI. The kingdom was believed to have witnessed another division in power between the pharaohs and the Theban high priests of Amun. It began when High Priest Amenhotep clashed swords with Panehesy, the viceroy of Kush. The priest was not a favorite among the Egyptians, possibly because of his hunger for power. He was ousted from office by his people, but his appeal to Ramesses was successful since he was reinstated to his former position. Unbeknownst to the priest, despite granting him the position, the pharaoh was also cooking up another plan to suppress his power. Ramesses XI requested Panehesy and his Nubian troops to march into Thebes, which eventually led to a siege of the priest's fortified temple of Medinet Habu.

Amenhotep's fate remains a mystery; it is unsure whether he survived the attack or if he simply retreated. However, the outcome of the battle was not what Ramesses XI had pictured mind since Panehesy went on to claim himself the de facto ruler of Lower Egypt. Ramesses XI sent an army led by another viceroy of Kush named Piankh against Panehesy. Despite successfully sacking the ancient city of Hardai (better known as Cynopolis) in Middle Egypt, Panehesy's forces were eventually defeated by Piankh and his army. He was then forced to retreat back to Nubia sometime around 1080 BCE. Ironically, after Panehesy's retreat, Piankh assumed the title of the high priest of Amun, thus starting wehem mesut, a period where high priests held power over Upper and Middle Egypt.

Ramesses XI was succeeded by Smendes, who founded the Twenty-first Dynasty, marking the beginning of Egypt's Third Intermediate Period—an era often described by many as the kingdom's darkest age since Egypt never fully recovered from this period. Much of Smendes's origins are unknown. Some suggest that he was once a governor in Lower Egypt under Ramesses XI, while others claim that he was somehow related to Herihor, the ruling high priest of Thebes. Nonetheless, Manetho stated that the first pharaoh of the Twenty-first Dynasty actively reigned over a divided kingdom (particularly Lower Egypt) from Tanis for twenty-six years. He died sometime in 1052 BCE and was succeeded by six more pharaohs, with Psusennes II being the last ruler of the Twenty-first Dynasty.

During the Twenty-second Dynasty, the highest power in Egypt was again passed to a foreigner, though all of them were pretty much culturally Egyptian. This time around, the throne belonged to rulers from the land of Tjemehu, better known to us today as Libya. Also referred to as the Bubastite dynasty (due to their main residence being at a location along the Nile called Bubastis), the very first ruler was believed to have ascended to the throne with little to no struggle. However, despite not facing tremendous opposition from the Egyptians, the king, Shoshenq I (who scholars claim to be the same person as Shishak from the Hebrew Bible), did not accept the responsibilities of a ruler empty-handed. He was an accomplished warrior and the head of the Libyan mercenary tribe called the Meshwesh. The king was exceptionally fluent in military skills and strategies. His most popular military campaign was the one in Palestine; inscriptions of his success and exploits can be found carved on the wall of the Bubastite Portal at the Temple of Karnak.

However, military prowess alone was not enough to ensure the kingdom operated without problems. Given how vast Egypt's territories were, Shoshenq I knew right away that he had to delegate his power to several of his most trusted people. So, the king sent his sons to different regions of Egypt to serve as governors. Although referred to as governors, their roles varied, with some even becoming priests of Amun in Thebes. As for Shoshenq I, he reigned for at least twenty-one years, passing the mantle to his son,

Osorkon I, whose deeds mostly focused on the many construction projects across the valley, though most of them are forever lost to us.

Many other kings rose to the throne and claimed their rights over the kingdom, while the seat of the high priest changed hands fairly often. Under the reign of Shoshenq III, the royal house was split into two. While rulers of the Twenty-second Dynasty continued to assert their power from Bubastis, the kingdom was introduced to the Twenty-third Dynasty, which gradually grew its influence in several regions of the Nile Delta. Although the two dynasties initially ruled together, they were soon caught up in conflicts, with the main reason being issues of succession. The many civil wars exploding across the valley resulted in an even more fragmented kingdom. There were separate monarchies ruling from different cities, such as Herakleopolis, Tanis, Hermopolis, Thebes, Memphis, and Sais. The political instability greatly weakened Egypt's borders, which allowed the Nubians in Kush to plan their next steps.

The Rise of the Kushite Empire

Nubia had come a long way since the end of the New Kingdom. Its power had been gradually increasing until the Kingdom of Kush was eventually formed. The kingdom was based in the capital city of Napata. However, the Nubians never had a chance to expand their grasp over Egypt due to the constant fights happening between the many tribes that existed within the kingdom. But everything changed when Egypt began to lose its grip, especially when the state was already divided.

Although known to have been involved in numerous battles and conflicts with Egypt, the Nubians admired the colorful Egyptian culture and tradition; even the Nubian king Kashta was believed to have mirrored Egyptian customs and religious beliefs during his reign. When the king's daughter was appointed as the god's wife of Amun, the highest-ranking priestess of the cult of Amun, Kashta began to plot his moves to further expand his influence. Through his daughter's significant position, Kashta was able to assert his power with minimal effort. He eventually took control of Thebes and, later on, parts of Upper Egypt.

However, the Kushites' power was strengthened under the reign of Kashta's son, Piye. The new king of Kush was described by many to be a religious man who believed that he was chosen by the chief god Amun to rectify Egypt's corruption. When he learned that a particular Libyan prince named Tefnakht had proclaimed himself the sole ruler of Egypt after driving the last king of the Twenty-second Dynasty out of Memphis and forming a union with rulers of several nomes in the Nile Delta, Piye decided that it was high time for him to act. He first set his eyes on Thebes.

The Kushite king sent his army up the Nile, where they were faced with ships carrying dozens of soldiers, each equipped with weapons meant for war. Without haste, the Kushites bravely advanced and emerged victorious. The Kushites were able to resume their initial plan, which was to enter Thebes. The troops continued on land with hopes of reaching the city of Herakleopolis. Nearing the city, the Kushites were yet again entangled in a battle involving Tefnakht's united forces. Although well prepared for war, the Kushites were stunned upon discovering Nimlot's participation in the battle. Nimlot, the ruler of Hermopolis, had initially sworn his allegiance with the Kushites, so his betrayal no doubt angered Piye. Nevertheless, according to Piye's victory stele, the Kushites massacred the coalition of Delta rulers, except for Nimlot, who managed to escape.

When the news of Nimlot's betrayal and escape reached Piye, the king did not waste any time to leave his seat of power in Kush and march into Egypt with his personal army in tow. Under his command, the Kushite king laid siege to Hermopolis for several months. Sensing his defeat on the horizon, Nimlot was said to have sent his wife to negotiate with Piye. No details survived that explain the negotiations between the two factions; however, we can be sure that Hermopolis submitted to the king after the siege, with Piye granting Nimlot forgiveness for his betrayal. With the fall of Hermopolis, other cities soon bowed down to the Kushite king, with some even offering tributes.

Piye proceeded to shift his focus to Memphis. Wishing to avoid more unnecessary bloodshed, the king offered the ancient city peace if it surrendered. However, the generous offer was declined, which led to another battle. This time, Piye faced an elite army of eight thousand men led by none other than Tefnakht himself. But luck was clearly shining on the Kushite king, as his forces emerged victorious and successfully captured Memphis. As for Tefnakht, he was said to have set out on another campaign against Piye to no avail. He was then left with no choice but to surrender and swear an oath of loyalty to the king.

Being a pious man, Piye immediately began the process of purifying the city. He sent guards to protect the Temple of Ptah and tended to the many shrines of the Egyptian gods. The king might have gone to the Temple of Ptah, where he was purified and anointed as the ruler of Egypt. With Memphis securely in his grasp, Piye soon received tributes from the remaining cities across the valley and the submission of a few other rulers.

After his successful conquest, Piye left Egypt and sailed back to his homeland, never to return again. He started Egypt's Twenty-fifth Dynasty; however, the control of Egypt was left in the hands of his vassals while he remained on the throne of Kush, ruling his own booming empire until his very last breath.

Chapter 10: Egypt under Assyrian Occupation

Gone were the eras of native Egyptians claiming the throne. Ever since the start of the Third Intermediate Period, Egypt was under the control of numerous foreign kings who claimed to be the living embodiment of the ancient gods. First came the Libyans, whose rule led to the kingdom's division. Soon after, Egypt witnessed the rise of the Kushites, who eventually ended a series of civil wars that had long plagued the valley.

Indeed, the campaigns launched by Piye resulted in many deaths and bloodshed, but the outcome was not all unfortunate. Shabaka, Piye's brother who succeeded him, was said to have admired and respected Egyptian culture just as much as his predecessors to the point where he preserved almost all of the Egyptian traditions during his reign. Aware of the close ties between the Egyptians and their religious beliefs, Shabaka appointed his own son as the high priest of Amun at Thebes. He would also be responsible for many reconstruction projects. To put it simply, Kushite Egypt flourished.

However, that was the case until a Kushite pharaoh named Shebitku came into conflict with the Assyrians. Egypt openly provided safe sanctuary to the rebels of Judah, who had revolted against their Assyrian overlords. Egypt's Twenty-fifth Dynasty never failed to provide support to the rebelling kingdom, which eventually led to a set of wars that were first launched by the Assyrian king,

Esarhaddon.

Esarhaddon's rise to power was far from peaceful. When his father, Sennacherib, died at the hands of his two sons, Esarhaddon embarked on a six-week-long civil war against his brothers. After he eradicated his father's murderers—including their associates and family members—he finally sat on the throne, just as Sennacherib had envisioned. And so, after having a crown placed on his head and successfully restoring Babylon and securing the empire's borders, Esarhaddon set his eyes on Egypt, which was always seen as a nuisance to the Assyrian Empire.

The Assyrian king launched a campaign against Egypt in 673 BCE. During this time, Taharqa ruled the Nile kingdom. Hoping to defeat Egypt in one fell swoop, Esarhaddon marched his troops quickly. This advance was described by historians as his greatest mistake; his army was exhausted from the march, causing them to lose focus on the battlefield. Because of that, Esarhaddon's forces were easily defeated by Taharqa right outside of the city of Ashkelon. The Assyrian king was left with no other choice but to return to his capital, Nineveh.

It took at least two years before Esarhaddon could finally breach the borders of Egypt. Sometime around early 671 BCE, the Assyrian king, after learning from his mistake of his past invasion attempt, marched his large army toward Egypt at a much slower pace. While passing through the city of Harran (a major Mesopotamian cultural and religious center), Esarhaddon supposedly received a prophecy involving his successful campaign against Egypt. The prophecy, combined with the great state of his army, could have possibly elevated the king's confidence. The Assyrians soon emerged victorious over Egypt.

Esarhaddon then led his army to the kingdom's ancient capital, Memphis. The Assyrian king did not hold back, as he sacked the city as soon as he arrived. He ordered the capture of the royal family who called Memphis their home. Taharqa's wife and children were among the captives sent to Nineveh as hostages. As for Taharqa himself, the pharaoh managed to slip out of the city and make his escape to the south in one piece.

Esarhaddon did not pursue Taharqa right away. Instead, he focused on consolidating his position in Egypt. After sacking

Memphis and capturing most of the royal family, the Assyrian king came up with a political reform for the northern regions of Egypt. Those who had been extremely loyal to Esarhaddon were chosen to be the governors of his newly conquered territories. An individual known as Necho I was named Egypt's new king, who ruled from his seat of power in Sais; however, some sources claim Necho I was nothing more than a puppet ruler.

With the riches that Esarhaddon had obtained from his successful campaign, he prepared for his return to the Assyrian capital. There, he erected a victory stele, which featured an image of Taharqa's son in chains. Statues of Taharqa were also brought back to Nineveh as trophies and placed at the entrance of the palace.

The Victory Stele of Esarhaddon.
Richard Mortel from Riyadh, Saudi Arabia, CC BY 2.0
<https://creativecommons.org/licenses/by/2.0>, via Wikimedia Commons:
https://commons.wikimedia.org/wiki/File:Victory_stele_of_Esarhaddon.jpg

Egypt, led by Pharaoh Taharqa, who had managed to evade the Assyrians, was not ready to submit to the Assyrians. So, in 669 BCE, another revolt led by the Twenty-fifth Dynasty pharaoh exploded just as soon as Esarhaddon left the kingdom. The news of this revolt reached the Assyrian king and immediately infuriated him. The king readied his army yet again and embarked on another campaign to quell the rebellion. Despite the king's strong will to defeat the rebels and finally put an end to Taharqa, the campaign was brought to a halt following the sudden death of Esarhaddon while he was still en route to Egypt. His death no doubt caused a stir in the Assyrian Empire, but this did not mean Egypt was safe from the Assyrians. Esarhaddon was succeeded by his son, Ashurbanipal, who would soon resume his late father's mission.

The state of the new Assyrian king's empire made it impossible for him to leave Nineveh. The empire constantly faced threats from the ancient Iranians (the Medes, Cimmerians, and Scythians). However, this did not stop the king from dispatching his troops to Egypt. The Assyrians clashed swords with Taharqa's forces near Memphis. The Kushite pharaoh faced defeat but yet again escaped to the south and found refuge in Thebes.

While pursuing the pharaoh, the Assyrians discovered that a few of the empire's appointed vassals who ruled Lower Egypt—including Necho I—were plotting to betray them. With haste, the conspirators were ordered to be captured. Some of the people over which they ruled were massacred; some were put in chains and deported to Nineveh. However, much to everyone's surprise, Necho I was pardoned and reinstated as the king of Egypt, while his son, Psamtik, was appointed as the mayor of Athribis, an ancient city in Lower Egypt. Taharqa fled to the Kushite capital of Napata, where he remained until his death. The Kushite kingdom was passed to possibly Taharqa's cousin, a man known as Tantamani.

Taharqa's death slightly calmed the conflict between Egypt and the Assyrian Empire but not for long. Tantamani, the new ruler of the Kushite kingdom, had only one wish: he wanted to restore his family to the Egyptian throne. Knowing that the Assyrian troops had returned to their capital, Tantamani grabbed the opportunity to march down the Nile and regain the territories lost to the Assyrians. He first reoccupied Aswan before advancing to Thebes and, finally,

Memphis, where he killed Necho I.

Necho I's death angered Ashurbanipal, which led to a renewal of the violent conflict. The Assyrian king, assisted by Psamtik I's army, which consisted of strong mercenaries from Caria, launched a massive attack against Tantamani in northern Memphis. The battle resulted in Tantamani's terrible defeat. Seeing no other way out, he fled to the south. The Assyrians chose to do the unthinkable: they marched to Thebes and sacked the city. Its inhabitants were put in chains and deported, the city's riches and gold were seized, and horses and two towering obelisks were brought back to Assyria. The Assyrians gained control of Egypt, with Tantamani's reign only limited to Napata. His death in 656 BCE ended both the Twenty-fifth Dynasty and the Nubian domination of Egypt.

The Twenty-sixth Dynasty began with Pharaoh Psamtik I, who succeeded to the throne after the death of his father, Necho I. Ruling the kingdom from Sais, the pharaoh was believed to have created a foundation for Egypt to bloom yet again. In an effort to unify the kingdom, the pharaoh formed an alliance with Gyges, the king of Lydia in Asia Minor, and raised an army that was made up of reliable Greek and Carian mercenaries. He then went on to deal with the unruly vassals and princes in the Nile Delta. To further consolidate his power, Psamtik I shifted his attention to Thebes, the holy city of Amun. He arranged the adoption of his daughter, Nitocris I, to Shepenupet II, the current god's wife of Amun. With his daughter next in line as the god's wife, Psamtik I expanded his power over the vast valley and held the state together. The pharaoh also gained popularity due to his encouragement of the revival of the Old Kingdom's religion and art.

Sometime in 653 BCE, Psamtik I gained even more autonomy, which was largely owed to Assyria's internal strife. He took this opportunity to break away from the Assyrians' hold, thus making him the sole ruler of Egypt. However, some sources claim that despite the Egyptian kingdom's detachment from Assyria, the pharaoh maintained a friendly relationship with the waning empire. For instance, Psamtik sent reinforcements to Assyria to repel the Babylonian attacks.

With Egypt completely in his hands, Psamtik I went on to bring Egypt back to its feet. He oversaw a great number of construction projects and was also responsible for the expansion of the Serapeum of Saqqara and the construction of fortresses at Daphnae, Naukratis, and Elephantine.

After over five decades, the mantle was passed to Psamtik's son, Necho II, who would soon be in the middle of Assyria's continuous conflicts. The declining empire had already lost its capital, Nineveh, in 612 BCE to the hands of a combined force of Babylonians, Medes, Persians, and Scythians. To retaliate, the Assyrians requested the help of the Egyptians, which Necho II granted. While marching toward the battlefield, the Egyptians likely met King Josiah of Judah's forces. Josiah had formed an alliance with Babylon. The king of Judah's plan to block the Egyptians' advance failed, as he was killed in Megiddo. With the path cleared, the Egyptians joined the Assyrians in Haran. However, they were swiftly defeated. The Egyptians retreated into northern Syria.

The fight, however, did not stop there, as they were left with no choice but to face the Babylonian army led by Nebuchadnezzar II (also known as Nebuchadnezzar the Great). This battle resulted in the defeat of the combined forces of Egypt and Assyria, with the latter ceasing to exist as an independent state. Despite Necho II's defeat against the Babylonian king, he continued to rule over Egypt and left a few great contributions to the kingdom. The pharaoh initiated the construction of a canal (also known as Necho's Canal), which later on became the blueprint for the Suez Canal. Necho II also recruited a great number of Ionian Greeks and formed an Egyptian navy, thus increasing the kingdom's shipbuilding activities, especially triremes.

After ruling over the valley for fifteen years, Necho II was succeeded by his son, Psamtik II. Psamtik II ruled Egypt for only six years, but he accomplished some significant achievements. To secure the valley from any possible invasion from the Kushites, Psamtik II launched an expedition into Nubia. He marched his troops as far as the city of Kerma and the Kushite capital of Napata; both cities were destroyed. With their capital city reduced to only ashes and rubble, the Kushites were left with no choice but to move their capital farther south toward the city of Meroe.

The following year, after Psamtik II's successful expedition against the Kush, he made a move to display his support for

Zedekiah, the king of Judah, who was preparing a revolt against the Babylonians. Although Zedekiah received reinforcements from Egypt, the revolt failed terribly, as Nebuchadnezzar II laid siege on the city for two years.

Psamtik II died sometime in 525 BCE, and the throne was passed down to his son, Apries. Like his father, the pharaoh became entangled in Palestinian affairs. He sent reinforcements to Jerusalem, hoping to assist the city in repelling the Babylonian forces under the command of Nebuchadnezzar II. Unfortunately, after an eighteen-month siege, Jerusalem fell. This resulted in the capture of the Jews. The nobles were held in captivity and sent to Babylon, while those who managed to escape migrated to Egypt.

Apries was also plagued with several more internal conflicts that eventually led to his own demise. While dealing with a civil war that broke out between the native soldiers and the foreign mercenaries, the pharaoh was forced to deal with his own general, Ahmose II, who was proclaimed by the Egyptian troops as the next king of Egypt.

When the news of the military coup reached Apries, the pharaoh fled to Babylon to seek support. He returned to Egypt in 567 BCE with an army of Babylonians to reclaim the throne. However, his advance failed. Apries was killed in battle, leaving the throne to none other than Ahmose II.

To further strengthen his position as the new ruler of Egypt, Ahmose II married one of Apries's daughters. Ahmose II, who was officially crowned as pharaoh, brought Egypt to its zenith. He built and restored numerous temples and structures across the valley, oversaw Egypt's agricultural growth, cultivated a close relationship with the Greek world, and defeated an invasion by the Babylonians in 567 BCE. He is regarded as one of the most powerful pharaohs of his time. But before his death, the pharaoh witnessed the early threats imposed by the rising Persian Empire.

Chapter 11: The Persian Conquest

The Persian Empire (known as the Achaemenid Empire at this point in time) owed its glory to none other than Cyrus the Great. Claiming the throne at the ripe age of only twenty-one, Cyrus was believed to have freed his city from the grasp of the Median Empire by orchestrating a successful revolt sometime in 549 BCE. However, his triumph over the king of the Medes was only the beginning of his conquests. He soon expanded his empire by launching campaigns in Lydia, which rewarded him and his empire with tremendous wealth. Cyrus later marched into Mesopotamia and conquered its surrounding regions.

In 539 BCE, the king was able to assert his power over the ancient city of Babylon without a single drop of blood being shed. The Babylonians were said to have welcomed Cyrus peacefully, as the king was not only popular for his military brilliance but was also a man of mercy; those who yielded were promised no harm and were allowed to practice their religious customs and traditions. He even liberated nearly forty thousand Jews, some of whom had been held in captivity for around fifty years.

An illustration of Cyrus the Great.

Arya.Go, CC BY-SA 4.0 <https://creativecommons.org/licenses/by-sa/4.0>, via Wikimedia Commons: https://commons.wikimedia.org/wiki/File:Cyrus_the_Great_II.jpg

It could be plausible that the great Persian king once sought to expand his power as far as Egypt, possibly because of the valley's invaluable economic resources. However, Cyrus never set foot in Egypt, as the king met his fate about a decade after his conquest of Babylon. Cyrus the Great was believed to have died in battle during his campaign against the defiant nomadic tribe known as the Massagetae. However, Egypt was not forgotten for long, as the valley would soon be forced to bow down to Cyrus's son and successor, Cambyses II.

The main reason for the first confrontation between Egypt and Persia is uncertain, but according to the Greek historian Herodotus, it all began during the reign of Ahmose II, a pharaoh from the Twenty-sixth Dynasty. Cambyses II was said to have requested for an Egyptian physician—some said he specifically asked for an ophthalmologist—to serve in his empire. Choosing to comply with the Persian king, possibly to avoid any tensions, the pharaoh forcefully ordered an Egyptian physician to move to Persia, thus leaving the doctor with no choice but to leave his wife and children behind. This no doubt angered the physician, who later planned to take down the pharaoh from afar. He established a good relationship with the Persian king before slowly injecting his malicious agenda. The physician suggested that the king ask the Egyptian pharaoh for his daughter's hand in marriage, which he claimed could result in a firm relationship with the Egyptians.

Upon learning of Cambyses's proposal to tie the knot with one of his daughters, the pharaoh grew wary. He refused to see his daughter as a concubine to a foreign king, but at the same time, the pharaoh wished to avoid any possible battle that could take place should he decline the Persian king's offer. And so, instead of sending his daughter, Ahmose II sent Nitetis, the daughter of his predecessor, Apries, who, according to Herodotus, was tall and beautiful. However, Ahmose's deception did not last long, as Nitetis chose to betray the pharaoh and informed Cambyses of her true lineage. The revelation angered the Persian king, which eventually led to his careful plans to invade the Egyptian kingdom.

Whether Herodotus's description of the story has any truth at all remains unknown. Nevertheless, Cambyses II spent years preparing for the Egyptian conquest. The way into the valley was indeed rough, and finding the best route proved to be rather difficult. However, thanks to Phanes of Halicarnassus, a mercenary and a wise tactician serving under Ahmose, the Persian king was able to perfect his strategy. Herodotus told us the mercenary was once loyal to the pharaoh until, for reasons unknown, he fell out of favor with Ahmose II and decided to leave Egypt for Persia. After successfully escaping his captivity that had been ordered by the anxious pharaoh who suspected his betrayal, Phanes of Halicarnassus arrived in Persia, where he eventually spoke with Cambyses II, who was in the midst of preparing the conquest. The mercenary made use of his knowledge of Egypt and advised Cambyses of the best way to enter the valley. He suggested the Persian king negotiate with the Arabian kings so that they would grant him safe passage to the Nile kingdom.

Holding hatred toward Ahmose, the Arabs gladly complied with the king's request and even supplied the Persians with fresh water and more troops. With a safe passage secured and aid from the Arabs, Cambyses II finally launched his campaign. However, his battle was not against Ahmose II since the pharaoh died six months before the Persian king could even set foot in the desert. Instead, Cambyses's rival was the new king of Egypt, Psamtik III, the son of Ahmose II.

Legend has it that a few days after the coronation of Psamtik III, the holy city of Thebes witnessed a sudden rainfall. It was a rare occurrence, and it was interpreted as a bad omen by the Egyptians. Perhaps it was a warning to the new pharaoh about the incoming attack from the Persians led by the vengeful Cambyses II. When news of the invasion reached Psamtik III, the young pharaoh immediately mounted a defense and spent days and nights preparing for the battle. Psamtik likely lacked enough experience on the battlefield, as he relied on the help of allies. He first sent his admiral, Udjahorresnet, to the Mediterranean coast to fend off the Phoenician fleet sent by Cambyses. Unfortunately, the admiral chose to turn his back on the young pharaoh and sided with the Persians. The same could also be said of his other ally, Polycrates of Samos; instead of supplying mercenaries to the Egyptians, Polycrates sent his men to join the ranks of Cambyses instead.

Despite having to face the betrayals of his allies, Psamtik III carried on with his defense strategy. The pharaoh held his ground at Pelusium, a major city on the easternmost branch of the Nile, and fortified his capital city, Memphis, hoping it could withstand a possible siege. Psamtik was said to have been quite confident about the battle, as, initially, his troops were able to hold back the Persians. However, the tide soon changed when the battle erupted at Pelusium. Cambyses, who had learned all about the Egyptians' customs and religious beliefs, especially their veneration for cats— cats were considered sacred to the Egyptians; they were often associated with the goddess Bastet—ordered his troops to paint their shields with an image of Bastet. Some sources even claimed that the Persians brought cats and other sacred animals onto the battlefield. Upon seeing the images of their goddess on the shields of their enemy and the sight of their sacred animals, the Egyptians sheathed their swords and attempted to retreat.

The meeting of Psamtik III and Cambyses II.
https://commons.wikimedia.org/wiki/File:Meeting_Between_Cambyses_II_and_Psammeti
chus_III.jpg

Herodotus claimed that despite the surrender, many Egyptians were massacred on the battlefield. Historians suggest that nearly fifty thousand Egyptians perished during the battle, while the Persians only lost seven thousand lives. Any of the Egyptians who survived the battle immediately retreated to Memphis; the young pharaoh was one of the survivors. However, the Persians were far from done, as they laid a siege on Memphis shortly after the Egyptian retreat. Psamtik III was taken prisoner following the successful siege. The pharaoh was said to have been treated fairly despite being a prisoner but was later executed when it was discovered that he was planning a revolt against the Persians.

Cambyses continued his campaign and marched his army throughout the valley. By 525 BCE, the Persians had conquered all of Egypt, with the neighboring Libyan tribes voluntarily submitting to the triumphant king. With the vast valley officially becoming a satrapy to the Persian Empire, Cambyses proceeded to Sais, where he finally crowned himself the new pharaoh of Egypt.

Adopting the pharaoh name of Mesuti Ra, Cambyses II founded the Twenty-seventh Dynasty of Egypt. However, according to Herodotus, the Persian king was the complete opposite of his father. While Cyrus the Great's greatest value was his mercy,

Cambyses II was known for his cruelty. The Greek historian even went to the extent of describing him as a stereotypical mad king.

Since the conflict between Egypt and Persia started during Ahmose II's reign, the Persian king was believed to have held grudges against him. When the pharaoh died before he could even arrive in Egypt, Cambyses decided to seek his revenge on Ahmose's preserved body. He trespassed in the pharaoh's tomb, stole his mummy, and burned it to ashes. Herodotus's most famous accusation of the Persian king was the slaying of the sacred Apis bull of Memphis.

CAMBYSES KILLING THE APIS.

Cambyses II slaying the Apis Bull.
https://commons.wikimedia.org/wiki/File:Cambyses_killing_the_Apis.jpg

Whether or not Cambyses did all those atrocious acts remains a debate, though most contemporary evidence suggests otherwise. The Persian pharaoh seems to have never dreamed of erasing Egyptian culture. His image might have been tarnished by the priests since the Persian king was not at all favored by them, possibly due to one of his opinions; in contrast to the native rulers of Egypt, Cambyses II thought that it was unnecessary for the kingdom to collect taxes from its subject just to support the temples.

The Persian pharaoh faced several revolts by the Egyptians during the first few years after the conquest. Other than Psamtik III, Cambyses was also forced to take down a resistance led by an individual named Petubastis IV sometime in 522 BCE. Upon learning of the revolt, Cambyses immediately sent his troops to quiet it down. The outcome of this battle is a mystery. Herodotus suggests that Cambyses's forces were defeated by Petubastis IV, but to cover up the failure, Cambyses claimed the troops were lost in a terrible sandstorm while marching toward the battlefield. Regardless of the outcome, the Egyptians never gained authority, and their kingdom continued to be governed by the Persians.

After Cambyses's death in 522 BCE, Egypt was reigned by the next Persian king, Darius I, who ruled for over thirty-five years. Despite having to experience numerous revolts across the Nile Valley, Darius was best known for his architectural contributions. Historians believe that, like the rest of the Persian pharaohs, Darius never sought to remove the unique cultures of Egypt. In fact, he worked on integrating Persian culture into the Egyptian culture. Under Darius I, the valley was introduced to the Persian water systems, which were more advanced compared to the ones familiar to the native Egyptians.

A relief of Darius I (also known as Darius the Great).
Surenae, CC BY-SA 4.0 <https://creativecommons.org/licenses/by-sa/4.0>, via Wikimedia Commons: https://commons.wikimedia.org/wiki/File:Darius_I_(The_Great).jpg

Darius I was succeeded by Xerxes I upon his death in 486 BCE. Xerxes I, who ruled for slightly over two decades, is best remembered for his attempt to annex Greece. He was assassinated by his own allies in court. The throne was left to his son, Artaxerxes I. During his reign, the Twenty-seventh Dynasty began to witness its first signs of decline. Artaxerxes's biggest challenge was Inaros, an Egyptian rebel who had formed an alliance with the Athenians.

To quell the rebellion, Artaxerxes dispatched an army commanded by the satrap Achaemenes. Perhaps luck was not on the Persians' side, as they were swiftly defeated by the rebels. The Egyptians regained their power over certain parts of the valley, although the Persians remained within the fortified walls of Memphis. However, six years later, the Persians gained the upper hand and defeated Inaros and his Athenian allies, resulting in Egypt falling back into the hands of the Persians.

Another rebellion soon broke out during the reign of Darius II, the last pharaoh of the Twenty-seventh Dynasty. The rebellion was led by an Egyptian who went by the name of Amyrtaeus. He and his followers successfully removed the Persian pharaoh from the throne and returned Egypt to the hands of native rulers. Darius II's successor in Persia, Artaxerxes II, likely made a move to restore the Persian occupation in the valley, but his efforts were cut short since he was forced to face a series of uprisings and revolts imposed by the angry Egyptians. Thus, the Egyptians managed to free themselves from the grasp of foreign rulers, ending the first period of Persian Egypt. However, this only lasted for a century since the Persians would return stronger than ever.

The second period of Persian occupation began after the reign of Pharaoh Nectanebo II. During the first years of his rule, Egypt prospered. The pharaoh also successfully protected his kingdom from numerous invasion attempts by the Persians with the help of his army and Greek mercenaries. However, things changed when the pharaoh was betrayed by a Greek mercenary named Mentor of Rhodes, who brought his men into the ranks of the Persian king, Artaxerxes III. With the support of a few Greek cities (except Athens and Sparta, which peacefully declined to go against Egypt) and Mentor's mercenaries, Artaxerxes III ultimately crushed Nectanebo II's forces in 342 BCE. After his victory, the Persian king marched to Memphis and installed a new satrap. Nectanebo II fled to Nubia and made plans to reclaim the throne, though his attempt was unsuccessful.

With Nectanebo II removed from the throne, Egypt was yet again put under the control of the Persians for the next decade. Artaxerxes III ruled until his death and was succeeded by Artaxerxes IV Arses and then Darius III, who would soon face Alexander the Great and witness the fall of the Persian Empire.

Chapter 12: Alexander the Great and the Ptolemaic Kingdom

Brilliant, diplomatic, charismatic, ruthless, hungry for power, and bloodthirsty—these are some of the words often used to describe Alexander the Great. The young conqueror was said to have never been alone, be it during the short times of peace or constant warfare. He was always accompanied by his loyal men who swore to follow him anywhere he ventured.

Before permanently carving his name into the history books as one of the greatest military minds of the ancient world, Alexander, like many other powerful historical figures, was born into a highly esteemed royal family. While some believe that he was the son of Zeus, the mighty king of the Greek gods, historians prefer another version. In 356 BCE, he was born to King Philip II of Macedonia and his wife, Queen Olympias. Although brilliance and prowess are not always inherited through the bloodline, it was a different case with Alexander. His father was an impressive ruler. Despite being left with a feeble country at the beginning of his reign, Philip II proved his exceptional commanding skills by molding his ineffective army into a formidable force. His determination to lift the kingdom out of its terrible state eventually came to fruition, as he subjugated most of Greece and transformed Macedonia into a force to be reckoned with.

Perhaps his father's victories sparked young Alexander's determination to display his vigor and bravery. In fact, the young conqueror shared the same fantasy as his father, which was to conquer the Persian Empire. At the age of twelve, Alexander proved his gift by taming Bucephalus, an enormous and furious stallion that many believed could be ridden by no one. The stallion soon became Alexander's most loyal companion in countless battles and wars.

At thirteen, Alexander began to absorb crucial knowledge from Aristotle. Three years later, he was temporarily left in charge of Macedonia when his father rode into battle. Before he was twenty, Alexander joined his father on the battlefield against the Sacred Band of Thebes, an elite force of the Theban army consisting of 150 pairs of male lovers. Some sources claim that Alexander's cavalry unit decimated the enemy troops and brought Macedonia another glorious victory.

Alexander the Great at the tomb of Cyrus the Great.
https://commons.wikimedia.org/wiki/File:Valenciennes,_Pierre-Henri_de_-_Alexander_at_the_Tomb_of_Cyrus_the_Great_-_1796.jpg

Two years after the victory, Alexander received news of his father's assassination at the hands of his bodyguard, Pausanias. With the passing of the forty-six-year-old king, Alexander rose to the throne as Macedonia's new ruler. After squashing his rivals, Alexander began to make a move on realizing his goal: to continue Macedonia's world domination plan and overthrow the Persian Empire once and for all.

Throughout the course of his vicious battles with the Persians, Alexander had one aim: eliminate the empire's ruler, King Darius

III. Only three years after claiming the throne, Alexander had the pleasure of going into yet another battle and facing the Persian king for the first time. King Darius III could breathe easy when he realized that Alexander was outnumbered by his tens of thousands of troops. His relief, however, was cut short when he witnessed the Macedonians' determination to take him down. Alexander was believed to have seriously injured his thigh, but his wound never slowed his advance. Darius III went from being confident of emerging victorious over the young conqueror to fleeing the battlefield in his chariot before switching to a horse.

Alexander the Great facing King Darius III at the Battle of Issus.
momo from Hong Kong, CC BY 2.0 <https://creativecommons.org/licenses/by/2.0>, via Wikimedia Commons:
https://commons.wikimedia.org/wiki/File:Alexander_the_Great_fighting_at_the_battle_of_Issus_against_Darius_III_of_Persia_(5886504798).jpg

Sources claim that Alexander went on to pursue the fleeing king until the sky darkened, but not even his tracks were found. The young conqueror only found the Persian king's mother, wife, and two daughters in Darius's private tent. As ruthless as Alexander could be, the Macedonian king refused to harm the women. Instead, he informed them of Darius's escape and promised them their safety since he was only after the dominion of Persia. Sisygambis, the mother of the Persian king, was deeply disappointed by her son's cowardice, which led her to plead her allegiance to the young Macedonian king. It is also believed the two unlikely allies formed a strong bond to the point where Alexander would refer to Sisygambis as his "mother."

King Darius III wished to regain his family and end the war peacefully, but his peace offering was immediately declined by Alexander. Alexander continued his campaign in Egypt, where he was left with no choice but to endure the time-consuming siege of Gaza. At the time, the city was protected by high walls reaching over sixty feet in height. Alexander and his men attempted three times before they could finally find a way to breach the walls and capture the city. Although the Persian commander of Gaza, Batis, had been terribly defeated, he refused to surrender to the young conqueror, which resulted in a terrible death. —the commander was dragged alive by a chariot around the city until he died.

The success of the siege left a door open for Alexander to enter Egypt and assert his power with little to no resistance. Witnessing the Persians' fall at the hands of the young Macedonian king, the Egyptians celebrated his arrival with open arms. At Memphis, Alexander was crowned with the double crown, symbolizing his power over Upper and Lower Egypt, thus making him the pharaoh of the kingdom. Under Egyptian tradition and belief, the new pharaoh was deified as the son of Ra and worshiped by most of his subjects.

While Alexander was said to have respected Egyptian culture and customs—he even went as far as to publicly honor the main Egyptian gods—the young conqueror was also aware of the riches of the Nile. He knew the exploitation of Egypt's resources could play an important role in his upcoming campaigns, especially his plans to track down King Darius III. Alexander initially chose Pharos as the site of his new city, then shifted his focus to another location on the edge of Egypt, which could be used to control trade between Egypt and the Mediterranean. Delighted with the location and after encountering good omens, the conqueror founded the city of Alexandria. Even though Alexander never lived to see the completion of the city, Alexandria soon turned into the center of Hellenistic culture.

A drawing of the ancient city of Alexandria.

Gnauth, Adolf, CC BY-SA 2.5 <https://creativecommons.org/licenses/by-sa/2.5>, via Wikimedia Commons: https://commons.wikimedia.org/wiki/File:Ancient_Alexandria_(1878)_-_TIMEA.jpg

Historians suggest that Alexander spent only six months in Egypt and brought the country back to its feet before embarking on another campaign. With Mesopotamia as his next destination, the conqueror finally clashed swords for the second time with King Darius III. Overwhelmed yet again, Darius fled the battlefield. However, his fate was already sealed, as his own troops assassinated him. Alexander replaced Darius as the new king of Persia and expanded his dominion. He marched to India in 327 BCE. Four years later, he planned his next move to invade Arabia, although this campaign did not come to fruition. The mighty conqueror died in June 323 BCE at the ripe age of thirty-two. Some believe that he died of malaria, while others claim he was poisoned. Nevertheless, Alexander the Great left no successors to inherit his vast empire, which included Egypt.

Ptolemy I Soter, Founder of the Ptolemaic Dynasty

Ptolemy was one of the successors of Alexander the Great and the founder of Egypt's Ptolemaic dynasty, which would thrive until the conquest of the Roman Empire. He was born sometime in 366 BCE, but not much is known about his early life; not even his family line was ever confirmed. While historians suggest that Ptolemy was born to a well-respected Macedonian nobleman known as Lagus, others also believe that he was the illegitimate son of King Philip II. However, this is nothing but a rumor, especially since scholars claim that Ptolemy was fond of exaggerations and would use such propaganda to further strengthen his position. Nevertheless, Ptolemy was, no doubt, a Macedonian general who was more or less important during the entire course of Alexander's conquests.

Despite being older than Alexander and the other generals who marched into Persia alongside him, Ptolemy received a full education and was tutored by Aristotle. It is safe to assume that he was close to the young conqueror even before he claimed the throne. Ptolemy participated in a number of battles, especially those against the Persians. Later on, Ptolemy, who was already serving as the young king's advisor, was given the honor of being Alexander's personal bodyguard.

Alexander was said to have clearly expressed his anger upon discovering the sudden death of King Darius III. When the identity of the assassin was revealed—Darius's second-in-command named Bessus—Alexander ordered Ptolemy to travel to a certain village where Bessus was about to be extradited by his officers. Following the king's orders, Ptolemy returned with Bessus, who was tied up and stripped naked. The assassin was flogged in public before having his ears and nose chopped off—a punishment common among the Persians. To end his misery, Bessus was sent to the ancient city of Ecbatana, where he was executed in front of Darius III's brother.

After the successful conquest of the Persians, Ptolemy continued to march alongside the young king. During the campaign in India, Ptolemy was said to have been seriously injured by a poisoned arrow. He was almost at death's door until Alexander saved his life by using a special brew made up of a combination of several native herbs. This might have been one of the reasons behind Ptolemy's loyalty to Alexander. However, after the death of Alexander in Babylon, Ptolemy and the other generals began to fight each other in hopes of securing power over the many lands within the vast empire.

A marble bust of Ptolemy I Soter.
Gary Todd from Xinzheng, China, CC0, via Wikimedia Commons:
https://commons.wikimedia.org/wiki/File:Marble_Bust_of_Ptolemy_I_%22Soter,%22_Fou
nder_of_Ptolemaic_Dynasty_of_Egypt,_c._3rd_C._BC_(28018907870).jpg

When Ptolemy accompanied Alexander to Egypt several years prior, the general was taken aback by the kingdom's rich resources. He saw the potential that Egypt had to become one of the most powerful nations in the world. When the self-proclaimed regent of the Macedonian Empire, Perdiccas, suggested they wait for the birth of Alexander IV (the son of Alexander the Great and his wife, Roxana) before they named the next ruler, Ptolemy was quick to portray his objections. After leading a campaign to divide the empire among the generals, Ptolemy managed to get his hands on Egypt. However, this was only the beginning of the Wars of the Diadochi, a conflict fought by Alexander the Great's main generals.

Although Ptolemy had already been named the governor of Egypt, he could not rest easy, as he knew that he was being watched by Perdiccas. So, he began plotting a grand theft. In the eyes of the

Macedonians, the remains of Alexander the Great were more than just a cold, lifeless body; they were the talisman of authority and legitimacy. Whoever had his remains held the true power of the empire. Ptolemy attempted to steal the king's body when his elaborate funeral cart left Babylon to head to Macedonia. After successfully bribing the escort, Ptolemy diverted the cart to Egypt. Alexander was laid to rest in Memphis, the governing center of Egypt at the time.

Perdiccas, whose power was severely tarnished without Alexander's body in his possession, soon planned an attack against Ptolemy in Egypt—a move that resulted in his demise. The majority of the Macedonian troops swarmed to fill the ranks of Ptolemy's army. With his plan a success, Ptolemy was finally free from Perdiccas, although he was soon involved in yet another set of wars between the rest of Alexander's power-hungry generals and successors. In 305 BCE, Ptolemy proclaimed himself the pharaoh of Egypt, and a year later, he gained the title "Soter" or "Savior" after defending the inhabitants of Rhodes from one of Alexander's generals, Demetrius I.

After the defeat of Antigonus, another one of Alexander's generals and the founder of the Antigonid dynasty, at the Battle of Ipsus, Ptolemy was finally able to shift his entire focus to Egypt. His first step was to move the capital of the kingdom to Alexandria, the golden city envisioned by Alexander the Great before his passing. Given the city's strategic location at the mouth of the Nile, a new trade route was established, which hugely benefited Egypt's economy. More Greeks began to flock to the city, thus making Greek the official language of the government and commerce.

Although Ptolemy did not learn the Egyptian language and spoke only Greek, he never abandoned the traditions and customs of his subjects. Priests were allowed to resume their daily religious activities, and temples that had been demolished by the Persians were reconstructed. In an attempt to assimilate Greek influences into the Egyptian religion, Ptolemy founded a new cult centered around Serapis, a deity born from both Egyptian and Greek beliefs.

Ptolemy also sought to transform Alexandria into the intellectual capital of the Hellenistic world. He commissioned the construction of a museum and the famous Library of Alexandria, which housed stacks upon stacks of papyrus scrolls and books of various precious knowledge. The king of Egypt was also responsible for the foundation of the Lighthouse of Alexandria, which was later completed by his son and earned its place on the list of the Seven Wonders of the Ancient World. The Pyramids of Giza also made it on the list.

Ptolemy founded a new dynasty and placed Egypt on the right track. The land prospered, with its wealth growing continuously. Its trade and economy flourished, and its borders were secure. The kingdom soon became desirable by many forces of the ancient world. After the king's death in 282 BCE, his direct descendants would continue to rule over the rich kingdom for nearly three centuries. But, of course, no kingdom was ever free from struggles for too long. Civil wars soon plagued the land, which eventually gave way for the Romans to gradually assert their power. Egypt was brought to its glory again under Cleopatra, but peace and independence were not meant to last in Egypt for much longer.

Cleopatra, the Last Ruler of the Ptolemaic Dynasty

Many are likely familiar with the name Cleopatra. She was one of the few queens of Egypt whose name is well known today. As one of the most controversial figures in ancient history, Cleopatra is often depicted as a power-hungry ruler who would do anything to secure her throne. However, contemporary evidence suggests that the queen of the Nile was one of the most powerful pharaohs of the dynasty.

Cleopatra spent most of her youth learning about the world. It is believed Cleopatra could speak at least six different languages, and she was the only Ptolemaic pharaoh who could speak Egyptian. She aided her father during his reign, so it should not come as too much of a surprise that the queen managed to bring Egypt into yet another era of prosperity.

Cleopatra's legendary meeting with Julius Caesar.
Jean-Léon Gérôme, oil on canvas, 1866., CC BY-SA 4.0
<https://creativecommons.org/licenses/by-sa/4.0>, via Wikimedia Commons:
https://commons.wikimedia.org/wiki/File:Cleopatra_Before_Caesar.png

However, her journey to claim the throne was not without its obstacles. When her father, Ptolemy XII, died, the mantle was passed to Cleopatra and her husband-brother, Ptolemy XIII. (Although there is no firm proof they married, it is likely they were since it was traditional for the Egyptian royals to marry their sibling.) Since Ptolemy XIII was merely a child when he rose to the throne, Cleopatra led the people. She even went to the extent of having only her face minted on the kingdom's currency. Only her name would be signed on official documents. This, no doubt, angered the young Ptolemy XIII; he claimed that Cleopatra was nothing more than a power-hungry ruler who sought to have the kingdom all to herself. And so, after gathering enough support, Ptolemy XIII successfully drove his sister-wife out of her homeland. Stripped of power by her own flesh and blood, Cleopatra sought refuge in Syria until an opportunity arose that could potentially assist in her mission to reclaim the throne.

A Roman civil war exploded between two Roman generals: Julius Caesar and Pompey. The war eventually brought the future queen of Egypt back to her feet. Pompey was killed upon Ptolemy XIII's orders. Caesar sailed to Egypt to confront Pompey and was mortified to learn that the great general had died in such a way. Caesar stayed in Egypt, hoping to use the civil war in Egypt to his own advantage.

Upon learning of Caesar's stay in Alexandria, Cleopatra planned for her grand but discreet entrance, hoping she could earn the Roman general's support and pave the way for her to reclaim the crown. According to legend, the future queen hid in a sack and sailed to the fortified city of Alexandria. Once they docked, Apollodorus carried the queen—who was still hiding in a sack—on his shoulder and made his way to the palace where Julius Caesar stayed. Cleopatra revealed herself to the Roman general and easily caught Caesar's attention and won his heart.

Cleopatra was able to reclaim the throne with the support of her new lover, despite her brother-husband's clear disapproval. It was said that the young pharaoh stomped his feet in anger upon finding Cleopatra in Caesar's chamber. However, Cleopatra was not one to let her enemies remain close to her. Ptolemy XIII soon died when he launched a war against Caesar.

The Egyptian throne now belonged to her alone. Cleopatra did marry another one of her brothers, Ptolemy XIV, but it was agreed that she would be the one responsible for state matters. Egypt flourished yet again. The kingdom was stabilized, and corruption was widely minimized. When drought and famine terrorized the valley, the queen fed her subjects food from her royal granary. Under Cleopatra, the kingdom rarely saw rebellions. Before another civil war could possibly happen, Cleopatra ruthlessly removed all of her siblings who displayed even the slightest signs of revolt.

However, things began to change when Caesar was assassinated in Rome. The queen, who was believed to have been in Rome during the incident, made haste to Egypt the moment news of the general's death reached her ears. A series of wars broke out in the

Roman Republic. Taking the opportunity to solidify her position and relationship with Rome, the queen forged a relationship with Mark Antony, one of the Roman Republic's greatest generals and a close ally of Julius Caesar. However, this move marked the beginning of her demise. According to several ancient Roman historians, Antony was becoming more Egyptian than Roman, which further fueled his rivalry with the future Roman emperor, Octavian (later known as Augustus).

The Romans believed the Egyptian queen had corrupted Antony with her wiles. So, the Romans declared war against Egypt. In the Battle of Actium, Cleopatra's and Antony's forces faced Octavian's troops in the Ionian Sea near the city of Actium. The naval battle, which took place in 31 BCE, resulted in the defeat of both Cleopatra and Mark Antony. Sensing their deaths were around the corner should they remain in battle, the two retreated to Alexandria. Octavian, who was insistent on ending the decades-long rivalry with Antony and removing Cleopatra from power, pursued them to the city and defeated the remaining Alexandrian troops.

A scene of the Battle of Actium.
https://commons.wikimedia.org/wiki/File:Castro_Battle_of_Actium.jpg

Seeing that victory was far from reach, Cleopatra committed suicide in August 30 BCE; Antony had already died beforehand due to a self-inflicted wound upon hearing a rumor of the queen's death. With the death of the last Ptolemaic queen, Egypt could no longer taste complete freedom, as the kingdom was annexed into the Roman Empire, which was formed by Augustus. This is considered the end of ancient Egypt. Egypt would be a part of Rome for over six centuries.

Chapter 13: Old Kingdom Art: Mummies, Figures, Temples, Reliefs, and Murals

An Egyptian man was preparing to leave his place of work and return to his home, where his wife and children were patiently waiting. However, the man's expression quickly changed when he was approached by his assistant, who informed him of the arrival of yet another dead body that required his immediate attention. The man, who had spent most of his life working as an embalmer, was left with no choice but to extend his working hours to tend to the poor body.

Working late was not uncommon for the ancient Egyptians, especially embalmers. Death was not a rare occasion in the kingdom of the Nile. After receiving the body, the embalmer began the early process of mummification. The corpse was placed on a low embalming table, with the person lying on their bare back. With the embalmer's assistant at his side, the embalmer cut an incision on the deceased's lower left abdomen. The embalmer then inserted his arm into the incision up to his elbow as he reached for the internal organs. He would first reach for the intestines and draw them out of the corpse before dropping them into a large pottery bowl. The bowl full of guts would be filled with natron, a type of preservative agent typically found in dry lake beds. Natron was the most important agent in the process of mummification since it was necessary to desiccate the corpse and its organs, preventing decomposition.

After the intestines, the embalmer moved on the liver; he would carefully jab and slice anything that held the liver together in the stomach before pulling it out and dropping it in another pottery vessel filled with natron. The same procedure was used when he moved on to retrieve the lungs. The only organ left inside the body was the heart. The ancient Egyptians believed the heart was the nucleus of a person's physical self, intelligence, and emotion. So, it was of the utmost importance to leave the heart untouched, though it might have been difficult to pull the heart out without damaging it.

The brain was seen as nothing more than a space filler in the skull. To remove the brain, the embalmer had to insert an iron hook into the nostrils until he could feel the soft surface of the brain itself. With the hook, he would then work to break the brain into tiny pieces and pull them out through the nostrils. Again, the embalmer would insert the iron hook through the corpse's nose and mash up the remaining parts of the brain until he could finally feel the hard walls of the skull. With the help of his assistant, the embalmer flipped the corpse over so that he could slap the back of its head to flush out the mashed brain, which would have turned into a thick liquid. Afterward, the embalmer poured tree resin into the skull to avoid further decomposition.

Once the body was free from all internal organs that could rapidly decay—aside from the heart, of course—the embalmer would then clean the rest of the corpse before moving it into a large jar filled with heaps of natron. The inside of the body was also filled with packets of natron to ensure thorough desiccation. The corpse was left entirely covered in natron for at least forty days. As for the internal organs that had been removed from the body, they were stored in separate limestone jars sealed with lids, each featuring the carvings of the four sons of Horus—Duamutef guarded the stomach, Hapi the lungs, Imsety the liver, and Qebehsenuef the intestines. These four jars would be interred along with the mummified corpse in its tomb.

Canopic jars representing the four sons of Horus.
https://commons.wikimedia.org/wiki/File:Canopic_jars_BM_4SoH.jpg

Forty days later, the embalmer would return to resume his work on the corpse. He would wash away the natron covering the body before stuffing linen rags into the incision to make the deceased appear more lifelike and fuller. False eyes were also added to ensure the corpse looked like how the person did while still alive. Now that the body was removed from all moisture and completely dried out, the embalmer would proceed to the final stage of mummification: wrapping the deceased. Using hundreds of yards of linen, he would carefully wrap the linen strips around the corpse while a priest recited prayers and spells for the soul of the deceased.

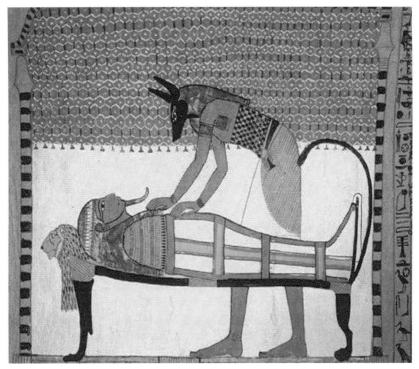

Anubis or a priest attending the mummy of the deceased.

https://commons.wikimedia.org/wiki/File:Anubis_attending_the_mummy_of_Sennedjem.jpg

The priests wore masks that resembled the god Anubis and would oversee the entire process to ensure a flawless mummification. When the mummy was finally completed, a mask would be placed over its wrapped head. The type of masks varied depending on the status of the deceased. Death masks belonging to a wealthy family were often covered in gold and exquisite paints, while those who were less fortunate could only afford simple masks with unembellished details. The same could be said for amulets; the rich would be interred with many amulets made out of precious stones, while the poor could only have a few amulets made of much cheaper materials.

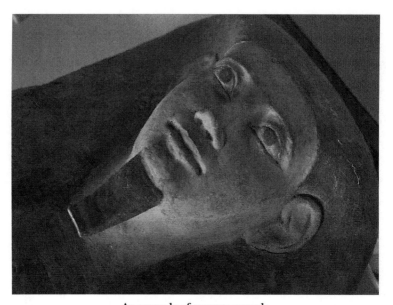

An example of a mummy mask.
Biswarup Ganguly, CC BY 3.0 <https://creativecommons.org/licenses/by/3.0>, via Wikimedia Commons: https://commons.wikimedia.org/wiki/File:Mummy-mask_-_Egyptian_Human_Mummy_-_Egyptian_Gallery_-_Indian_Museum_-_Kolkata_2014-04-04_4424.JPG

The entire mummification process took seventy days. Once done, the mummy would be ready to be interred within their tombs, which had been built and designed beforehand. Elaborate burial practices took place to ready the deceased to move on to their next life. Most of the time, the mummy was placed inside a sarcophagus before getting interred in their burial chamber. The entrance would then be sealed.

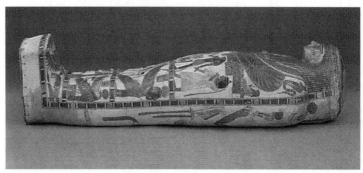

An example of an Egyptian coffin.
Art Institute Chicago, CC0, via Wikimedia Commons:
https://commons.wikimedia.org/wiki/File:Coffin_and_mummy_of_Paankhenamun_03.jpg

The interior of an Egyptian coffin.

Slices of Light, CC BY-SA 4.0 <https://creativecommons.org/licenses/by-sa/4.0>, via Wikimedia Commons: https://commons.wikimedia.org/wiki/File:%22Yellow_Coffin%22_-_Ancient_Egyptian.jpg

Figures and Statues

The Egyptians of the Old Kingdom were undoubtedly ahead of their time, especially when it came to sculptures. The Great Sphinx of Giza is the greatest example of their extraordinary work. Believe it or not, the ancient Egyptians never once referred to the great sculpture as the Sphinx. It actually owes its name to the Greek travelers who thought the sculpture resembled a mythical being, the female-headed Sphinx. This was possibly due to its body resembling a lion and the Nemes on its head (a stripped linen headcloth worn by pharaohs), which was mistakenly thought to be the hair of a woman. It was only referred to by the Egyptians of the Old Kingdom as *shepsepankh* (which simply means "living image"), although people in the New Kingdom called it Horemakhet ("Horus in the horizon").

The Great Sphinx of Giza.

English: Taken by the uploader, w:es:Usuario:BarcexEspañol: Tomada por w:es:Usuario:Barcex, CC BY-SA 3.0 <http://creativecommons.org/licenses/by-sa/3.0/>, via Wikimedia Commons: https://commons.wikimedia.org/wiki/File:Great_Sphinx_of_Giza_-_20080716a.jpg

The reason behind the construction of this magnificent structure remains debated by scholars. However, many agree that it was somehow erected to honor the pharaoh Khafre because the Sphinx's head closely resembles the pharaoh. Certain parts, particularly the features on the face of the Sphinx, are no longer perfect, but through careful observations and studies, Egyptologists managed to reimagine the sculpture back to when it was at its utmost glory. From the stone fragments scattered between the Sphinx's paws, it is plausible that the sculpture once had a beard—

the one typically seen on a pharaoh's statue. There were also traces of paint behind the ears, which might indicate the Sphinx was initially adorned with paint on its face. Last but not least, it is safe to assume the sculpture sports a Nemes, the blue and gold striped linen headdress worn by the pharaohs.

Why Khafre wanted his image combined with the body of a lion remains a mystery. Since felines, especially cats, were considered sacred animals by the ancient Egyptians, it is plausible that the great pharaoh wished to be seen as a divine entity, perhaps just like the gods themselves. Nevertheless, it is the construction of the Sphinx that intrigues us the most. Scholars have long agreed that besides being master builders, the Egyptians were amazing geologists. They knew how to exploit their surroundings to their advantage, and the Sphinx was a great example of that. Instead of building the Sphinx's body above the ground, archaeologists believe that the Egyptians actually dug trenches into the bedrock, thus exposing the layers of limestone underneath. From there, wooden wedges were used to separate the layers and carve out the rough shape of the Sphinx. The spoils of the limestone layers were then recycled and used to build surrounding temples. The stonemasons then worked their magic. With their copper chisels, they added the details of the pharaoh's face and carved the lion's body.

However, the many elaborate statues and figures scattered throughout the lands of the Nile did not always serve as decorations or signs of power. More often than not, they played a role in the ancient Egyptian religion. A ka statue, for instance, was crucial for the souls of the deceased. The Egyptians believed that, upon dying, the soul was released from the body, allowing it to roam the world. However, the soul needed its own permanent physical body to return to after roaming the world of the living. Ka statues were created for this very purpose. To ensure the spirit or *ka* recognized their resting place, wooden or stone statues were erected with the likeness of the deceased. Ka statues of a pharaoh usually featured a Nemes. The statue of a pharaoh also had a false beard, which signified their status as a living god. Since ka statues are classified as funerary art, they were often found in burial tombs.

An example of a ka statue.
Jon Bodsworth, Copyrighted free use, via Wikimedia Commons;
https://commons.wikimedia.org/wiki/File:Ka_Statue_of_horawibra.jpg

While ka statues were reserved especially for the pharaohs, the royals, and the rich, the tombs of those belonging to non-royals often featured a type of sculpture referred to as reserve heads. In contrast to the ka statues, reserve heads were rather simple and plain. These busts featured neither hair nor a specific headdress. Despite being considered a ka statue for the commoners, the true purpose of the reserve heads remains uncertain; some scholars claim that they merely served as portraits.

Egyptian Stelae

Unlike the Greeks and the Romans, Egyptian stelae could often be seen on the walls of a temple or tomb. The earliest appearance of an Egyptian stele can be traced back to the First Dynasty at Abydos. In contrast to those in later periods, stelae from the First Dynasty were rather simple; they featured only the title and name of the tomb owner. By the time of the Second Dynasty, these stelae began to appear more complex. One of them had an image of an individual sitting on a chair surrounded by various offerings. One of the reasons the Egyptians included a stele within a tomb was to keep the memories of the deceased alive.

Stele of the scribe Iry.
Szilas, CC0, via Wikimedia Commons:
https://commons.wikimedia.org/wiki/File:Stele_of_the_scribe_Iry,_Gulbenkian_Museum.j
pg

During the Old Kingdom, false door stelae were the norm. These carved false doors were believed to have been used by the souls of the dead as a passageway to the living world. Through this door, the dead would be able to access the offerings left by those who were still breathing.

A common false door in an Egyptian tomb.
Louvre Museum, CC BY-SA 3.0 <https://creativecommons.org/licenses/by-sa/3.0>, via Wikimedia Commons: https://commons.wikimedia.org/wiki/File:Louvres-antiquites-egyptiennes-img_2947_cropped.jpg

As time passed by, stelae evolved into not only serving as a form of decoration in a tomb or a passageway for the souls of the dead but were also used to commemorate a specific event or victory.

The Sun Temple

The sun god Ra had always been one of ancient Egypt's most important deities, but he gained tremendous popularity during the

Old Kingdom. During this time, Ra was seen as the state deity. Due to Ra's rising importance, the Old Kingdom pharaohs commissioned the construction of temples to honor the sun god. Although Egyptologists believe more than a dozen sun temples were built in the valley, only two survived the test of time, with one of them being in Abu Gorab, just north of Abusir.

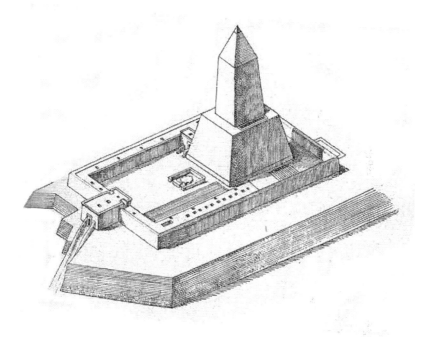

A drawing of the Niuserra's sun temple.
https://commons.wikimedia.org/wiki/File:Temple-solaire-abousir.jpg

Built sometime around 2430 BCE, the temple was also known as the Sun Temple of Niuserra. Based on the ruins, archaeologists can confirm that the temple once had three different sections, with one of them being the upper temple, complete with a 36-meter-tall obelisk, a four-sided square-based structure topped with a triangular pyramid. Obelisks were a symbol of the sun god. Directly in front of the tall structure was an altar, which was made out of white alabaster blocks. Purposely placed to be exposed to the sun, the altar was arranged to form a particular symbol that meant "Ra is satisfied."

Apart from the structures, various reliefs were carved onto the walls of the temple. One of them explained Ra's main role as the giver of life, while two other reliefs known as the "Chamber of the

Seasons" depicted the changing seasons of inundation and harvest. However, these two reliefs are no longer at Abu Gorab, as they were removed and put on display in a museum in Berlin.

A mural on the wall of the temple depicting an agricultural scene of ancient Egypt.
Osama Shukir Muhammed Amin FRCP(Glasg), CC BY-SA 4.0
<https://creativecommons.org/licenses/by-sa/4.0>, via Wikimedia Commons:
https://commons.wikimedia.org/wiki/File:Fowling_with_a_dragnet,_agricultural_scene,_an
d_handling_ducks._Wall_fragment_from_the_Sun_Temple_of_Nyuserre_Ini_at_Abu_G
urob,_Egypt._c._2430_BCE._Neues_Museum.jpg

Due to unknown reasons, the temple was destroyed several times, possibly by Mother Nature. Fortunately, it was restored by Ramses II during his reign in the New Kingdom era.

Chapter 14: Middle Kingdom Art and Customs: Life, Death, and Beyond

We know the ancient Egyptians were obsessed with life in all its forms; to them, even death was a new form of life. However, death was far from being merciful enough to end one's peril and troubles. In death, the Egyptians were expected to go through a journey filled with obstacles and threats before they could finally achieve peace or, rather, the Field of Reeds, where their needs would always be met.

A depiction of the Field of Reeds on a papyrus.
https://commons.wikimedia.org/wiki/File:Bookofthedead-fieldofreeds.jpg

Legend has it that in order to reach eternity, the Egyptians needed some help to navigate the paths of the underworld. Back in the Third Dynasty, they believed that only their kings and pharaohs had the ability to ascend toward the heavens. To guide their deceased ruler and protect them from the impending dangers on their path, the Egyptians often included many spells and incantations on the pharaoh's sarcophagus and on the walls of his pyramid. These religious texts are more popularly known as the Pyramid Texts.

Sometime toward the beginning of the First Intermediate Period, this exclusivity began to fade away. The Egyptians began to believe that the afterlife was no longer only limited to the royals; even commoners were allowed to ascend to the next life. And so, the Pyramid Texts began to evolve into what we know today as the Coffin Texts. Since ordinary individuals were now thought to be worthy of a continued existence, it was a must for them to have their own coffins to ensure they were buried with spells and incantations that could save them in the netherworld. The number of spells varied, and the inscriptions were not only limited to coffins, as they were also written on tomb walls, stelae, and sometimes the deceased's death mask.

The Coffin Texts painted on the interior of a coffin.
British Museum, Copyrighted free use, via Wikimedia Commons;
https://commons.wikimedia.org/wiki/File:Coffin_of_Gua.jpg

The Egyptian beliefs about life after death varied slightly as the kingdom progressed into the Middle Kingdom era. However, their burial customs underwent some changes. During the Eleventh Dynasty, it was common for the Egyptians—typically those belonging to wealthy families—to build their tombs within the mountains of Thebes and as close as possible to their pharaoh's tomb. Thebes was the main location for burials since it was the city of the Eleventh Dynasty kings. By the Twelfth Dynasty, the people had begun to change their preferred burial sites. The Egyptians, especially those who served in the pharaoh's office, were interred in mastabas located in Lisht, which was in close proximity to the capital of Itjtawy. The Pyramid of Senusret can still be found in Lisht today, though it has been severely damaged over the years.

What remains of the Pyramid of Senusret in Lisht today.
https://commons.wikimedia.org/wiki/File:Licht-senwsPyramids_01.jpg

As for those who belonged neither to the royal family nor the rich, their tombs appeared rather simple. Some were mummified and wrapped entirely in linen, while others were only wrapped but not mummified. The bodies of commoners were covered by cartonnage mummy masks, which were made out of layers of linen and plaster. Unlike the royals and high officials, who had the privilege of being interred in intricate sarcophagi gilded in gold, ordinary individuals could only afford to be buried in simple wooden coffins.

Since the Egyptians believed in life after death, it was not unusual for them to include different types of food items and even weapons in the tombs of the dead. Bread, a leg of beef, and beer were among the most common offerings found within the Egyptian tombs. Wooden models, such as boats, scribes, and soldiers, were also buried with the dead. Shabti, a type of figurine, was also commonly buried with the deceased; they were believed to be able to serve the deceased in the afterlife. This custom somehow mirrored the ancient Egyptian retainer sacrifices, when servants were sacrificed following a pharaoh's death to ensure they could serve their king in the next life. These sacrifices were only widely practiced during the First Dynasty and were eventually replaced with the shabti.

Examples of shabti figurine.
Metropolitan Museum of Art, CC0, via Wikimedia Commons:
https://commons.wikimedia.org/wiki/File:Shabti_of_Khabekhnet_and_Iineferty_MET_D T202025.jpg

The most popular item was a piece of jewelry or amulet called the heart scarab. However, it must be noted that jewelry was rarely included in the tombs of commoners. Just as its name suggests, the heart scarab was a type of amulet in the shape of a scarab, which is part of the beetle family. The heart scarab represented Khepri, the ancient god who could renew life. The funerary amulet was usually placed on a mummy's chest, and its purpose was to protect the heart of the deceased.

A heart scarab with inscriptions.
Brooklyn Museum, CC BY-SA 2.5 <https://creativecommons.org/licenses/by-sa/2.5>, via Wikimedia Commons: https://commons.wikimedia.org/wiki/File:WLA_brooklynmuseum_Heart_Scarab_late_9_t o_early_8th_century_BCE.jpg

Since the heart was considered the seat of a human's intelligence and emotions, it was a must for the Egyptians to ensure the once-beating organ remained unscathed until they finally passed through the Hall of Judgment, where their heart would be weighed against the feather of Ma'at. If their heart were damaged during the process of mummification, the heart scarab would act as a stand-in and be weighed against the feather. The amulet also played an important role during the final test in the Duat (the realm of the dead). Since the heart scarab was inscribed with a specific spell, it could prevent the heart from speaking against the soul of the deceased before the divine judges.

Architecture

The flourishing era of the pyramids might have belonged to the rulers of the Old Kingdom. However, when the Old Kingdom ended shortly after the death of Pepi II, with Egypt being ushered into its first dark era, the construction of pyramids started to become a thing of the past. The First Intermediate Period was so chaotic that the Egyptians saw a decreasing number of new pyramids being built in the valley.

By the time of the Middle Kingdom's Twelfth Dynasty, Egypt witnessed the resurgence of pyramids that resembled those from the Old Kingdom. However, the quality of these structures was, of course, average, especially compared to the magnificent pyramids at Giza. The pyramids of the Middle Kingdom were constructed with materials of lower quality. Instead of limestone blocks, many of the structures built during this time were made out of mudbricks, which explains the destruction of the pyramids in Lisht.

Amenemhat I was the first pharaoh who initiated the construction of a pyramid during the Middle Kingdom. He commissioned his pyramid complex in the necropolis of Lisht, which was not far from his seat of power in Itjtawy. Measuring at least 54 meters (177 feet) tall, the pyramid of Amenemhat I was built using a mixture of limestone blocks, mudbricks, and stones recycled from older pyramids. The entire structure was coated with limestone cladding to help sustain the unpredictable weather.

Inspired by the designs of the Sixth Dynasty, Amenemhat I had the entrance to the inner chambers built in the northern section of the pyramid, where one could find the offering hall. A tunnel that descended to an antechamber right underneath the apex of the pyramid was also built. From the antechamber was a vertical shaft that led straight down into the burial chamber, which is now submerged underwater due to the rising groundwater level. It is believed that the pyramid housed twenty-two burial shafts with at least four mastabas.

Unfortunately, the pyramid of Amenemhat I became a target for desperate grave robbers. Combined with the unpredictable weather of Egypt, what is left of the pyramid today is nothing more than ruins.

The Black Pyramid, commissioned by Pharaoh Amenemhat III, is another example of Middle Kingdom architecture. The pyramid got its name from the dark color of the exposed mudbrick core and was said to have been the first of its kind to house both the pharaoh and his queens. (The commoners often had monogamous marriages, while the pharaohs often had multiple wives to strengthen Egypt's diplomatic relations.) The pyramid also had complex interconnected passageways, which are believed to have been built to confuse tomb robbers. Some also suggest that the design had a ritual significance.

Nevertheless, like the pyramid of Amenemhat I, the Black Pyramid is in a poor state today, although its poor state is due to multiple errors made during its construction. The ground where the pyramid's foundations stood was unstable, and due to its location close to the edge of the Nile, parts of the pyramid flooded after the construction was completed.

What remains of Amenemhat III's Black Pyramid today.
Tekisch, CC BY-SA 3.0 <https://creativecommons.org/licenses/by-sa/3.0>, via Wikimedia Commons:
https://commons.wikimedia.org/wiki/File:Black_Pyramid_of_Amenemhat_III.JPG

Perhaps the most remarkable piece of architecture from the Middle Kingdom was another one of Amenemhat III's pyramids. Although the pyramid at Hawara failed to withstand the test of time—it currently resembles nothing but a huge mound—it was once a massive temple complex that gained the attention of many. Dubbed the Labyrinth, the ancient Greek historian Herodotus said the complex was awe-inspiring, largely because of its maze of rooms and winding passages. Unfortunately, like the pyramid itself, the temple complex was destroyed, leaving us with nothing but only small remnants.

Statues

Statues and sculptures no doubt reached new heights of technical perfection when Egypt was ushered into the flourishing period of the Middle Kingdom, particularly during the reign of Pharaoh Senusret III. Senusret III is often acknowledged as one of Egypt's most powerful pharaohs of the Twelfth Dynasty. He was popular for his supreme military prowess, but he was also known for his sculpture. The pharaoh's sculpture, which was made out of red granite, was unlike the ones carved during the reigns of his predecessors. Instead of sporting a youthful and vigorous appearance, the pharaoh had his sculpture capture his striking features as an aging king—a portrayal that deviated from the standard way of representing reigning Egyptian kings. Scholars have interpreted this portrayal as a way to symbolize the burden of kingship.

Statues of Senusret III.
British Museum, CC BY-SA 3.0 <http://creativecommons.org/licenses/by-sa/3.0/>, via Wikimedia Commons: https://commons.wikimedia.org/wiki/File:ThreeStatuesOfSesotrisIII-RightProfiles-BritishMuseum-August19-08.jpg

Colossal statues also began to be widely used during the Middle Kingdom. These types of statues were often erected in pairs and used to flank the main entrances of Egypt's many grand temples. The colossal statues were thought to have served as guardians of sacred temples and complexes. The best example of a colossal statue built during this period is the Seated Statue of a Pharaoh. The colossal statue, which was carved out of granodiorite, is believed to have represented either King Amenemhat II or Senusret II.

Many innovations in creating sculptures were introduced during the Middle Kingdom. The most prominent example of their flourishing art is the block statue, which managed to maintain its popularity until the Ptolemaic dynasty two thousand years later. This type of sculpture often featured a man sitting on flat ground with both of his knees drawn up to his chest. His two hands were folded and rested on top of his knees. To create the block-like shape, these sculptures wore a simple yet wide cloak, which at times covered their feet. While the shape of the statue's body appeared rather simple, the head of the sculpture included fine details.

These statues were mostly used as funerary monuments for important individuals. The reason behind the creation of block statues varies. Some suggest that the statue simply portrayed a man resting, while others claim that it had a deeper religious meaning involving the process of rebirth.

The colossal seated statue of Amenemhat II.
Juan R. Lazaro, CC BY 2.0 <https://creativecommons.org/licenses/by/2.0>, via Wikimedia Commons: https://commons.wikimedia.org/wiki/File:Amenemhat_II.jpg

Literature

The Middle Kingdom also witnessed the birth of the Egyptian formal writing system, which was often used in religious scripts, administrative documents, and literary works. One of the types of text used during this era was known as hieratic. Historians describe this form of writing to be some sort of cursive Middle Egyptian hieroglyphs. This language writing system was believed to be much simpler compared to the normal hieroglyphs that we are familiar with today, and writing in Hieratic was also faster, which was useful for producing larger works of literature.

Perhaps the most impressive literary work ever produced in the Middle Kingdom was the "Tale of Sinuhe," whose author remains a mystery, though he was probably considered the "Shakespeare" of ancient Egypt. It tells the story of Sinuhe, an assistant of Pharaoh Amenemhat I. Upon the king's death, Sinuhe was said to have been shrouded with fear and decided to flee from Egypt and start a new life somewhere near Syria, where he joined a tribe called the Bedouins.

The tale gives its readers a unique insight into the afterlife, as well as the details of the cultural differences between Egypt and the Near East. After imposing a self-exile and living as a Bedouin, Sinuhe grew a beard and had long hair, which was not acceptable according to Egyptian standards, as the elites were expected to be clean-shaven and neat. The tale also explores the main character's life journey, from when he first fit into a new tribe, his challenges with the warriors, and his longing to return to his place of origin, the kingdom of the Nile.

The "Tale of Sinuhe" has been studied by many scholars all over the world, and it is still unsure whether the tale tells the story of a real individual or is strictly fiction, though the locations, rulers, and cultural details described in the text are accurate for the time period. Nevertheless, this tale is agreed to be one of the oldest written forms of storytelling, as it was produced nearly four thousand years ago.

Chapter 15: New Kingdom Art: Innovations and Alterations

While civil wars, famine, plagues, and drought were some of the most common unfortunate events that terrorized the kingdom, the ancient Egyptians also had to deal with one particular crime: tomb robbing. Although tomb robbing had long been recognized as ancient Egypt's number one crime—tomb robbers already existed in the kingdom as early as the Predynastic Period—by the Second Intermediate Period, it had gotten even worse. The most targeted tombs were, of course, the pyramids belonging to the pharaohs and their royal family. The rulers of the kingdom tried to discourage the robbers by constructing confusing mazes and passageways in their pyramids or scattering debris all over the chambers, but these efforts failed to curb the crime. Many tombs were successfully broken into, and all of their precious treasures were looted, including the mummies of the pharaohs themselves.

As Egypt ushered in the booming era of the New Kingdom, the third ruling pharaoh of the Eighteenth Dynasty, Thutmose I, decided to change the funerary tradition for the pharaohs and the royal family. Instead of burying the deceased in a massive pyramid visible to the eyes of many from far away, the rulers of Egypt were interred in hidden tombs carved in the crags of the mountains of western Thebes. This burial site is known to us today as the Valley of the Kings.

The Valley of the Kings.
Fotograf/Photographer: Peter J. Bubenik (1995), CC BY-SA 2.0
<*https://creativecommons.org/licenses/by-sa/2.0*>, *via Wikimedia Commons:*
https://commons.wikimedia.org/wiki/File:Luxor,_Tal_der_K%C3%B6nige_(1995,_860x605).jpg

The reason behind its location was never confirmed; however, it could be plausible that the pharaoh chose this site as the new necropolis due to the highest peak of the Theban hills, El Qorn, which resembled the pyramids built by his predecessors. Others have suggested that it was because of the land's condition, as the area had always been barren. Not a single plant could be seen emerging from the ground. Because of this, the land would remain isolated. No one would ever think of establishing a new settlement nearby.

The peak of El Qorn.
Marie Thérèse Hébert & Jean Robert Thibault from Québec, Canada, CC BY-SA 2.0
<*https://creativecommons.org/licenses/by-sa/2.0*>, *via Wikimedia Commons:*
https://commons.wikimedia.org/wiki/File:%C3%89gypte,_Vall%C3%A9e_des_Rois,_N%C3%A9cropole_th%C3%A9baine,_El-
Qurn_(la_Corne)_montagne_pyramidale_dominant_la_vall%C3%A9e_(49834286528).jpg

With the perfect location in mind, Thutmose laid out his idea of a secret underground tomb to one of Egypt's renowned architects at that time, Ineni. He was believed to be responsible for many major construction projects from the reign of Amenhotep I until Hatshepsut and Thutmose III. According to the architect's own tomb inscription, he claimed that he oversaw the construction of Thutmose's hidden tomb alone. However, sources suggest he used foreign captives to work on the tomb. Once the construction was finished, they were killed so that the location of the pharaoh's tomb remained a secret.

Nevertheless, Thutmose's plan to secure his tomb and possessions was a success. The necropolis had only one entrance, so it was impossible for tomb robbers to enter the valley unseen. With that, Thutmose I successfully made a great change in terms of the burial traditions of the Egyptian rulers. Their tombs were rarely broken into, and their precious possessions remained by their side. This can be seen in Tutankhamun's tomb, which was discovered by archaeologists in near-perfect condition.

Although his tomb is considered by many to be evidence of ancient Egypt's vast wealth, with his near-perfect mummy gifting Egyptologists with a clear insight into the mummification process, Tutankhamun (more famously known as King Tut) was not the most remarkable pharaoh. He rose to the throne at the age of nine, and shortly after his succession, he changed his name from Tutankhaten to Tutankhamun. This was largely due to his well-known reformation of Egypt's religious traditions.

With the crown on his head, the young pharaoh erased his father's, Akhenaten's, footsteps. King Tut encouraged his people to abandon Aten, the sun god introduced by his father, and revived the worship of Amun, thus bringing back the centuries-old religious traditions of Egypt. Despite being revered by the Egyptians for restoring their religious beliefs, his name was almost completely forgotten the moment he died ten years after his succession. King Tut was a frail pharaoh. He suffered from multiple diseases all his life, possibly caused by inbreeding.

Although Tutankhamun was forgotten, his name soon became widely known throughout the world in 1922 when his tomb was discovered by the British Egyptologist Howard Carter. However, certain sources claim a twelve-year-old boy named Hussein Abdul Rasul accidentally stumbled upon the tomb's entrance while he was fetching water for the archaeologists. Nevertheless, when words of the tomb's discovery hit the public, the world was astonished.

Within the tomb are four separate chambers, with all of its precious contents and murals intact. The antechamber contained all of Tutankhamun's prized possessions, including some of the items he possibly used on a daily basis, such as three intricately crafted golden animal couches and a paper fan. There was also the burial chamber, where the young, sickly king was laid to rest. His intact mummy was accompanied by two statues of Anubis, the god of funerary rites and the fierce guardian of tombs and graves. The walls surrounding his sarcophagus were painted with different scenes of the young pharaoh interacting with the Egyptian gods.

Although the size of Tutankhamun's tomb was noticeably smaller compared to those belonging to other pharaohs before him, the large number of untouched treasures discovered within all four chambers of the tomb surely stunned many archaeologists. Over five thousand artifacts were found, most of which were made out of gold. To the ancient Egyptians, these treasures were stored within the tomb to accompany the soul of the deceased pharaoh in the afterlife, but for us today, they serve as a guide for us to journey back in time.

The interior of Tutankhamun's tomb.
EditorfromMars, CC BY-SA 4.0 <https://creativecommons.org/licenses/by-sa/4.0>, via Wikimedia Commons: https://commons.wikimedia.org/wiki/File:Inside_Pharaoh_Tutankhamun%27s_tomb,_18th_dynasty.jpg

The Book of the Dead

The tradition of burying the dead with everyday items had long been practiced by the Egyptians, and it continued even when the kingdom entered a whole new era. Sandals, pottery, weapons, furniture, and cosmetic objects were some of the most common grave goods included in the tombs of the ancient Egyptians. However, in contrast to the Second Intermediate Period, the grave goods became even more elaborate during the New Kingdom, possibly due to the kingdom's growing wealth after centuries of disarray. Aside from precious jewelry, the Egyptians, typically those belonging to the elite classes, included a particular item in their tombs that served as a guide for them to continue their life after death and safely reach the Field of Reeds.

Known as the Book of the Dead, this funerary text was written on a long piece of papyrus and contained a set of unique spells that had the ability to protect and navigate the deceased through the Duat. With this book, one could get a detailed insight into what to expect after death and how to pass each test posed by the gods who were waiting to judge their deeds.

The Book of the Dead was prepared by the Egyptian scribes after being commissioned by the relatives of the deceased. However, this was not always the case, as there were many who would commission the funerary text in advance to prepare for their own funeral. Although the Book of the Dead was considered vital to ensure a smooth journey in the Duat, not everyone had the privilege to have one interred in their tomb. The production of the funerary text was rather expensive. Laborers had to save almost half of their annual pay to afford the scroll, which was why the Book of the Dead was often only included in the tombs of the rich.

The contents and magic spells in the scroll—typically written in cursive hieroglyphs—varied from one person to another. As of today, historians have discovered 192 different spells, which were used for a wide range of purposes. The best-preserved Book of the Dead is the Papyrus of Ani. It granted Egyptologists a great detail of information on ancient Egyptian beliefs of the afterlife.

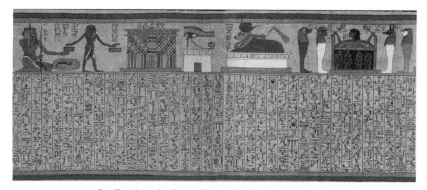

Spell written in the scribe Ani's Book of the Dead.
https://commons.wikimedia.org/wiki/File:Bookofthedeadspell17.jpg

The seventy-eight-foot scroll was believed to have been prepared for Ani, a scribe who once called the ancient city of Thebes his home. According to the manuscript, the journey through the Duat was daunting. The deceased must first pass through a series of dark caverns, lakes of fire, and magical gates guarded by nothing but the most fearsome of beasts, including Apep (Apophis), the mythical demon serpent that lurks in the darkness waiting to devour the souls who pass in front of him. Ani was saved from these threats since he had specifically customized his scroll to fit his spirit's needs. With incantations, prayers, and spells, the Egyptians believed Ani was able to repel the dangers scattered on his way and arrived at the Hall of Judgment. At this particular hall, Ani had to stand before forty-two gods who would assess his life on earth.

A depiction of the weighing of the heart.
https://commons.wikimedia.org/wiki/File:Egypt_dauingevekten.jpg

Ammit, the devourer of the heart.
https://commons.wikimedia.org/wiki/File:Ammit_BD.jpg

After proclaiming his good deeds and convincing the gods of his righteous ways, Ani then moved on to the weighing of the heart. This trial was one of the most daunting parts of the underworld. If his heart weighed heavier than Ma'at's feather—signifying his many wrongdoings—then it would be devoured by Ammit, a terrifying beast with the head of a crocodile and the body of a leopard and hippopotamus, thus ending his existence forever. However, thanks to Ani's righteous deeds, he passed the judgment and was granted passage to meet Osiris, who later gave him his approval to enter the Field of Reeds, a realm without pain, sadness, and anger.

The Temple of Hatshepsut: One of the Most Elaborate Temples of the New Kingdom

Despite the hatred of some Egyptians, Hatshepsut led Egypt into a prosperous period. Her expedition to Punt was the success that she was most proud of, but her biggest contribution is still visible today: her mortuary temple in Thebes. The pharaoh sought to immortalize the story of her life and power and was said to have commissioned the construction of her temple shortly after her ascension to the throne. The design and grand layout of the temple were Senenmut's ideas. Senenmut was Hatshepsut's steward and is also believed by certain historians to have been her lover.

Inspired by the Mortuary Temple of Mentuhotep II, which was also located in Thebes, Hatshepsut's grand temple had a massive stone ramp that connected the first courtyard to the second and third levels. The two temples portrayed numerous similarities, but Hatshepsut's was even more elaborate and surpassed the grandeur of any other temple built before.

The Mortuary Temple of Hatshepsut.

Marc Ryckaert, CC BY-SA 4.0 <https://creativecommons.org/licenses/by-sa/4.0>, via Wikimedia Commons: https://commons.wikimedia.org/wiki/File:Hatshepsut_Temple_R01.jpg

Back in ancient Egypt, the courtyard featured a lush garden, which visitors had to walk past before being welcomed by a set of two lion statues flanking the entrance of the central ramp. Upon reaching the second level, visitors continued to feast their eyes on the impressive sights of the reflective pools and statues of sphinxes lining the pathway that led to yet another ramp to the third level. While the complex was adorned with dozens of murals and reliefs, one could also find a tomb belonging to Senenmut.

Hatshepsut believed she had a special connection with Hathor and did not forget to include a temple to honor the goddess. On the opposite side of the Temple of Hathor was the Temple of Anubis, which was a common feature of a mortuary temple.

The entrance to Hathor's temple.

Olaf Tausch, CC BY 3.0 <https://creativecommons.org/licenses/by/3.0>, via Wikimedia Commons: https://commons.wikimedia.org/wiki/File:Totentempel_Hatschepsut_Hathorkapelle_12.jpg

Perhaps the most impressive part of the temple was the two colonnades standing on each side of the ramp leading to the third level. Located on the right side of the ramp was the Birth Colonnade, which featured a story of Hatshepsut's divine birth. Inscriptions on the walls of this colonnade claimed she was born after the god Amun had a sexual relationship with her mother. While the Birth Colonnade was built to tell her subjects of her divine birth origins, the Punt Colonnade on the left side of the ramp focused on her popular expedition to the land of Punt. According to the inscriptions, this expedition was not only welcomed by the people of Punt but also rewarded Egypt with exceptional wealth. Hatshepsut claimed that no king before her had ever brought the kingdom as much fortune as she did.

The Hypostyle Hall at Karnak, an Architectural Wonder Filled with Records of History

The Karnak Temple Complex was thought to have been developed during the Middle Kingdom. The complex was initially commissioned to be smaller; however, as Thebes gained more importance among the Egyptians, many kings began to leave their marks on the complex and instructed several great temples to honor the king of the gods, Amun-Ra—his temple was said to have been the earthly dwelling place for the god—and the gods Mut and Montu. As time went on, Karnak transformed into a wondrous complex complete with Egypt's most elaborate temples, a sacred lake, and other additional structures often used by priests, such as workshops and kitchens.

The central column of the Great Hypostyle Hall.
René Hourdry, CC BY-SA 4.0 <https://creativecommons.org/licenses/by-sa/4.0>, via Wikimedia Commons: https://commons.wikimedia.org/wiki/File:Temple_de_Louxor_53.jpg

However, out of all the magnificent structures located within the vast complex, the Great Hypostyle Hall attracted the most visitors. The hall was initiated by Pharaoh Seti I. It was not difficult to spot the hall since it consisted of 134 massive stone columns, with twelve of them towering over twenty meters high. Judging from the traces of paint that survived on certain parts of the columns, it is plausible that the hall was once painted in vibrant colors.

Apart from being an architectural wonder, the hall also served as a historical record. In the northern part of the hall, one can find the reliefs that depict the battles fought by Seti I. The southern section of the hall was completed by Ramesses II, so his contributions to the kingdom were carved on the walls. This included the Egyptian-

Hittite treaty that the king signed during his reign. Seti I and Ramesses II were not the only ones who had their successes recorded on the hall's walls, as later pharaohs would engrave their victories on the surfaces of the great hall as well.

Abu Simbel, Ramesses II's Proudest Construction Project

Rediscovered in 1813 after being covered by desert sands, Abu Simbel is one of the world's most impressive temples built by humans. The temple was constructed by Ramesses II to commemorate his victory at the Battle of Kadesh. Within the complex, one can find two different temples. The Great Temple, which took nearly twenty years to complete, was built to honor the pharaoh and the gods Amun, Ra, and Ptah. The second and smaller temple was constructed for the pharaoh's wife, Nefertari, and to honor the goddess Hathor. The most prominent feature of this temple is its entrance; the rock-cut gateway is flanked by four colossal seated statues of Ramesses II.

The entrance of the temple flanked by four statues of Ramesses II.
https://commons.wikimedia.org/wiki/File:Abu_Simbel_Temple_May_30_2007.jpg

The entrance to the smaller temple of Nefertari.
https://commons.wikimedia.org/wiki/File:Nefertari_Temple_Abu_Simbel_May_30_2007.jpg

Apart from the impressive architectural design, the temple also served as a great example of the ancient Egyptians' expertise in mathematics and astronomy. The site and position of the temple were chosen for a specific reason; the ancient Egyptians had perfectly positioned the temple to align with the sun so that the light would illuminate a particular chamber within the Great Temple on certain dates. Within the central chamber, one can find the statue of Ramesses II sitting alongside the gods Amun, Ra, and Ptah. Due to the temple's alignment with the sun, light only shines on the statues of the pharaoh, Amun, and Ra—Ptah's statue remains in the shadows since he is the god of darkness. This only happens twice a year: on February 21st, which was the date of Ramesses's coronation, and October 21st, which was the pharaoh's birthday. Throughout the rest of the year, the chamber is dark. This bi-annual event is known as the Sun Festival and continues to be celebrated today.

However, due to the rising water of the Nile, the temples recently had to be relocated. The painstaking relocation project took place in 1968 and was completed five years later. The temple and all of its structures were carefully dismantled and relocated about 180 meters away from its original site. Because of the change in its location, the dates of the Sun Festival have been moved to a day later. Today, visitors can witness the sun illuminating the chamber every February 22nd and October 22nd.

The relocation of the temple.
https://commons.wikimedia.org/wiki/File:Abusimbel.jpg

The sun illuminating the statues of Ramesses II, Amun, and Ra.
Diego Delso, CC BY-SA 4.0 <https://creativecommons.org/licenses/by-sa/4.0>, via Wikimedia Commons: https://commons.wikimedia.org/wiki/File:Templo_de_Rams%C3%A9s_II,_Abu_Simbel,_Egipto,_2022-04-02,_DD_26-28_HDR.jpg

Chapter 16: Ptolemaic Art

After driving the Persians out of Egypt and peacefully proclaiming himself as the new king, Alexander the Great was thought to have immediately shifted his focus toward constructing his own city. The city of Alexandria turned into one of the most visited Mediterranean cities. It was filled with an array of architectural wonders, most of which were unfortunately destroyed and lost to us forever.

The most prominent structure built during the Ptolemaic era was the Lighthouse of Alexandria, which was built by the first ruler of the Ptolemaic dynasty, Ptolemy I Soter. Named one of the Seven Wonders of the Ancient World, the lighthouse once proudly stood on the small island of Pharos, which faced the city's harbor. The lighthouse towered over a hundred meters (over three hundred feet) above sea level and was considered one of the tallest structures ever built in the ancient world, second only to the Great Pyramids of Giza. Just like any other lighthouse, the Lighthouse of Alexandria was built with the intention of guiding sailors across the vast Mediterranean Sea. The Egyptian coast was dangerous; it had sent many ships to the bottom of the sea. Thus, the lighthouse was necessary to warn sailors of shallow waters or even submerged rocks.

Besides serving as a navigational aid, some sources suggest that the colossal lighthouse was also constructed to honor the ancient gods, particularly Zeus or Poseidon. Ancient descriptions tell us that the lighthouse once featured a statue at the top, which many historians believed to have been the statue of the mighty Zeus.

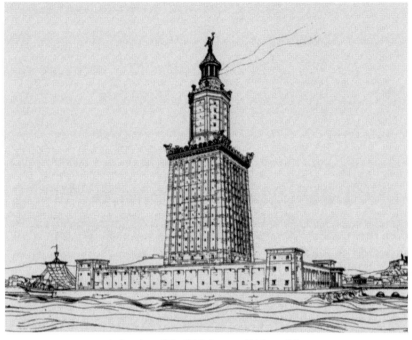

A drawing of the Lighthouse of Alexandria.
https://commons.wikimedia.org/wiki/File:Lighthouse_-_Thiersch.png

But none of the ancient writings that survived describe the exact design of the lighthouse. By piecing together all of the vague descriptions, it is safe to assume that the lighthouse had three different levels. The base was rectangular in shape, while the middle was octagonal, and the top was round. When night came, a fire would be lit at the top of the lighthouse. Ancient descriptions claimed that in order to make the fire visible to sailors from a distance, the Egyptians used a burnished bronze mirror to reflect the blazing flame.

The great lighthouse witnessed a few disasters and went through several reconstruction projects and repairs, but it stood on the small island for at least 1,600 years. In the 14th century CE, the lighthouse was no longer mentioned in the historical record. The Lighthouse of Alexandria was presumably destroyed sometime in the 1330s CE, although it has continued to leave its mark on us today.

The only remnants of the lighthouse found in the Mediterranean Sea.
Roland Unger, CC BY-SA 3.0 <https://creativecommons.org/licenses/by-sa/3.0>, via
Wikimedia Commons: https://commons.wikimedia.org/wiki/File:AlexLighthouse01.jpg

The Library of Alexandria

Being a student of Aristotle himself, it is not surprising to learn that Alexander the Great was very fond of knowledge. He wanted his city to become not only a center for trade and commerce but also for all knowledge of the world. Although he was never given a chance to see the completion of Alexandria, his dreams were eventually realized by his loyal general, Ptolemy I. Named the cultural and intellectual center of the Hellenistic world, the city welcomed countless visitors from all over the globe, particularly those from the Mediterranean. The greatest of Greek minds flocked to the city for one reason: to visit the Library of Alexandria.

An illustration of scholars studying in the Library of Alexandria.
https://commons.wikimedia.org/wiki/File:Ancientlibraryalex.jpg

The library was believed to have been nestled in the royal district of the city and integrated both Greek and native Egyptian cultures in its design. Grand Hellenistic columns might have been its most prominent features and were possibly accompanied by a great number of Egyptian statues. Unfortunately, no sources survived that give us an idea of the great library's exceptional design. We do know that inside the library were several lecture halls, classrooms, laboratories, meeting halls, gardens, and perhaps even a zoo. The library had rows of shelves, each filled with thousands of scrolls containing the world's most precious knowledge.

In the beginning, the shelves contained only Greek and Egyptian scrolls. The rulers of the Ptolemaic dynasty then began to actively invite many scholars to the city, which eventually resulted in the contribution of many more manuscripts. However, even this was not enough in the eyes of the Ptolemaic rulers, as they wished to own a copy of every book in the world. So, the rulers took advantage of Alexandria's port, which was bustling due to trade. A new policy was introduced that stipulated all ships that docked in

Alexandria had to hand over their books for copying. This responsibility was given to the library's scribes, who would spend their day duplicating the texts. The original copy of the manuscript was stored in the library, while the duplicated version was returned to the ships. Book hunters were also hired to travel the world in search of new books and writings. Ultimately, hundreds of thousands of scrolls and manuscripts were housed in the Library of Alexandria.

Of course, like many other structures of the ancient world, the Library of Alexandria failed to withstand the ravages of time. The library witnessed destruction in 48 BCE when Julius Caesar laid siege to the city. However, some sources suggest that only parts of the library were destroyed. Regardless of how much of the library was destroyed, it was restored and continued to be the hub of knowledge for years to come. We do not know when the library finally crumbled to the ground, but many claimed that its popularity began to decline during the Roman Empire.

Serapeum of Alexandria

After welcoming the reign of yet another dynasty, the Egyptians saw the birth of a new cult that soon gained popularity: the cult of Serapis. Scholars agree Ptolemy I made an effort to further integrate the ancient religion of the Egyptians with that of the Greeks. Ptolemy was well aware that it was nearly impossible for the Egyptians to accept a new and foreign deity into their traditional religion. So, he combined the two most popular Egyptian deities at the time—the lord of the underworld, Osiris, and Apis, who had been gaining popularity among the Greeks since the Twenty-sixth Dynasty—with the Greek god of lightning, Zeus. With the creation of the new god, Ptolemy began another rigorous building program. He commissioned the construction of the Serapeum, which would later be continued by his son and successor, Ptolemy II.

A marble bust of Serapis.
https://commons.wikimedia.org/wiki/File:Serapis_Pio-Clementino_Inv689_n2.jpg

Considered by many to be one of the grandest and most beautiful temples in Alexandria, the Serapeum was situated in the southwest of the city, right on a hill overlooking the sea. The temple was also referred to as the "Daughter Library," possibly because of its large collection of books. The Serapeum of Alexandria was believed to have been so big that visitors were required to climb hundreds of steps just to reach its magnificent courtyard. Its porticoes never failed to impress visitors, as they were beautifully adorned with gold and gilded bronze. However, the inner temple became the main highlight of the structure, as this was the very place where one could find the colossal statue of Serapis himself.

Since the Greeks were never fond of animal-headed gods, Serapis was always depicted as a bearded man dressed in a robe. His statue in the Serapeum was accompanied by Cerberus, the three-headed dog that guarded the gates of the Greek underworld. The god's right hand rested on the beast while his other hand held an upraised scepter.

Despite being worshiped after the Roman conquest of Egypt, Serapis was gradually abandoned when Christianity emerged. The Serapeum of Alexandria was destroyed by the Romans sometime in 391 CE. All we can see of this once-grand temple are broken ruins.

The ruins of the Serapeum of Alexandria.
Daniel Mayer, CC BY-SA 4.0 <https://creativecommons.org/licenses/by-sa/4.0>, via Wikimedia Commons: https://commons.wikimedia.org/wiki/File:Alexandria - Pompey%27s Pillar - view of ruins.JPG

Temple of Edfu

The Ptolemaic dynasty contributed to the construction of numerous extravagant temples, including the Temple of Kom Ombo, the Dendera Temple Complex, and the Temple of Esna. However, the best-preserved temple from this dynasty was located on the western bank of the Nile. Known as the Temple of Edfu, this particular temple had a huge difference compared to the ones often found in the Ptolemaic ruler's capital city: it had only little to zero Hellenistic influences. This massive temple surprisingly remained intact.

The Temple of Edfu had a few significances that made it important to the Egyptians. In terms of religious significance, the temple was constructed in honor of Horus and his beloved wife, Hathor, who was the ancient Egyptian goddess of fertility and love. After the temple's completion, it was believed that it immediately became the center of various ceremonies and celebrations involving the two divine entities.

The main entrance of the Temple of Edfu.
Patrick.reb, CC BY-SA 3.0 <https://creativecommons.org/licenses/by-sa/3.0>, via Wikimedia Commons: https://commons.wikimedia.org/wiki/File:Temple_Edfou_Egypte.jpg

The temple is also known for its series of hieroglyphs. One can take a step into the temple and feel as if they were transported into a book filled with thousands of writings telling different stories of the beliefs and myths from the Hellenistic period. Carvings of Egyptian writings adorned every corner of the temple, from the flat walls to the dozens of columns, chambers, and sculptures. These hieroglyphs are known as the Edfu Texts, and most of them tell the story of the creation of the world. From these texts, we know the ancient Egyptians believed the world started as an island created by the gods who descended from the skies. They also believed the gods built the first temple in the world, which soon became a blueprint for every temple that ever existed, especially the ones in the Nile Valley. Apart from the creation myth, the temple also featured texts describing the legendary feud between Horus and Set.

The Temple of Edfu fell into disuse when pagan and non-Christian worship was banned by the Roman Empire. The temple witnessed a series of destructions, which were typically perpetrated by the Christians who dominated the valley. We can see some of it today, such as the blackened ceiling of the temple's Hypostyle Hall. Centuries later, the temple was completely abandoned until it was eventually buried beneath the sands. However, this played a big role in the temple's near-perfect preservation.

Sculptures and Statues

Historians believe the artistic styles during the Ptolemaic era varied, especially during the reign of the dynasty's first few pharaohs. Perhaps due to political reasons, the sculptures of the early Ptolemaic pharaohs almost resembled those from the Thirtieth Dynasty; sometimes, the pieces from the two periods had so many similarities that Egyptologists faced difficulties distinguishing between them.

However, as time went by, the Ptolemaic statues began to abandon the old style of the previous dynasties and incorporate a hint of Greek influence. Despite still being depicted in an Egyptian pose (either seated or standing with their left foot forward), statues of the elite began to appear with curly hair, which was often seen in Greek-style art, and a full garment instead of a bare torso. Beards were also a common feature; the best example can be found on the statues of Serapis, the god of healing and fertility.

A statue of Serapis currently in the Vatican Museum.

Immanuelle, CC BY-SA 4.0 <https://creativecommons.org/licenses/by-sa/4.0>, via Wikimedia Commons: https://commons.wikimedia.org/wiki/File:The_Nile_Vatican_Statue.jpg

The statues of the Ptolemaic era were also finely carved and appeared to be more realistic compared to the typical Egyptian statues, which preferred a stiff and idealistic look. The Egyptians did not strive to achieve likeness when it came to statues and sculptures. But the Ptolemies were heavily influenced by the Greeks, so their sculptures emphasized the face more. Each feature was carved to be as realistic as possible, and the subjects were often portrayed with a smile that gave the statues a more reserved expression.

A bust of Ptolemy wearing a smile.
Stella, CC BY-SA 4.0 <https://creativecommons.org/licenses/by-sa/4.0>, via Wikimedia Commons:
https://commons.wikimedia.org/wiki/File:British_Museum_Egypt_-_Tolomeo_I.png

However, the most prominent change in Ptolemaic art was the reappearance of female statues, a form of art that had been abandoned since the Twenty-sixth Dynasty. The reason behind this was uncertain, but historians believe it was probably due to the rising importance of women during the Ptolemaic dynasty. Several female royals held important positions in the kingdom, with many becoming co-regents to the ruling pharaohs and some rising to the throne themselves. Although statues of women were rarely portrayed with the same realism as male statues, they still appeared with a hint of Greek influence. Arsinoe II (the wife of Ptolemy II) was often portrayed as Aphrodite, the Greek goddess of love. To infuse some Egyptian influence, her statue wore the traditional crown of Lower Egypt, the feathers of an ostrich (the symbol of the goddess Ma'at), or other traditional Egyptian headdresses and garments indicating royalty or a divine being.

Head of a statue of Arsinoe II.
Metropolitan Museum of Art, CC0, via Wikimedia Commons:
https://commons.wikimedia.org/wiki/File:Head_Attributed_to_Arsinoe_II_MET_DT10849.jpg

The Ptolemaic period also saw the birth of a statue that depicted a younger version of the god Horus, though some sources claim the statue made its appearance during the Late Period (the last era of native Egyptian rulers). Known as Harpocrates (a Hellenization of the Egyptian name Har-pa-khered, which simply means "Horus the Child"), the god was often represented as a young, nude boy with a sidelock of hair. He typically held one of his fingers up to his mouth—a realization of the Egyptian hieroglyph for the word "child," which was later mistaken by the Romans to be a symbol of silence and secrecy. To signify his divinity, the statue also wore a crown featuring a uraeus, a rearing Egyptian cobra.

A silver statuette of Harpocrates.
Patrick Clenet, CC BY-SA 3.0 <http://creativecommons.org/licenses/by-sa/3.0/>, via Wikimedia Commons: https://commons.wikimedia.org/wiki/File:Harpocrates_gulb_082006.JPG

Conclusion

With the shocking death of Cleopatra and her lover, Mark Antony, in 30 BCE, Egypt was left without a ruler. Its borders were soon breached by the future Roman emperor Augustus, who rode with his troops and claimed the vast kingdom. Before taking her own life, the last Ptolemaic queen was believed to have sent Caesarion, her only son with Julius Caesar, away from the dangers of the war, hoping he could survive and one day claim the Egyptian throne.

However, Cleopatra's wish was cut short, as Augustus ordered Caesarion's assassination to remove any future threat. Cleopatra's children with Mark Antony were spared by Augustus and sent to Rome, where they were left in the care of Augustus's sister, Octavia. Although the emperor tried to erase the traces of the two figures, he did grant them a proper burial. Cleopatra wished to be buried right next to Antony. However, the location of their tombs remains a mystery.

Egypt was immediately annexed into the Roman Republic after the defeat of Cleopatra. Although the kingdom's immense wealth was absorbed and eventually became the emperor's possession, Augustus was wise enough not to disturb the ancient Egyptians' old way of life, including their religious beliefs and traditional customs. The most prosperous periods of Egypt might have been a thing of the past, but Egypt no doubt managed to maintain its presence and spread its influence to every corner of the world, something it continues to do today.

Architecture and construction skills aside, the ancient Egyptians were renowned for their mastery of medical science; even the Persians agreed with this statement, as they once requested an Egyptian physician to move to their empire and share his knowledge. Many Egyptian medical texts have been discovered, each describing various medical information and surgery procedures in great detail. They were responsible for the invention of toothpaste. Back in ancient Egypt, dental issues were common. To curb the problem, the Egyptians experimented and developed several recipes for a substance to clean their teeth. One of the texts that survived the time tells us the ancient Egyptians made toothpaste using rock salt, mint, dried iris petals, and pepper. Surely, their methods and techniques had flaws, but the Egyptians were the precursors to modern medicine. Once a center of knowledge and education, it is not surprising to discover that the ancient Egyptians also laid the foundations for various other fields, such as language, astronomy, and mathematics.

Of course, ancient Egypt's most prominent influence on the world is its art and architecture. Several of the kingdom's most impressive buildings and colossal statues still stand today, and their ability to survive thousands of years amazes almost everyone. The pyramids inspired many contemporary and modern architectural works; the Louvre in Paris features a glass and stainless-steel pyramid that is heavily inspired by the Great Pyramid of Giza, while Harrods' Egyptian Hall in England is filled with the recreations of the pyramids, the Sphinx, and Egyptian columns, complete with the complex carvings of hieroglyphs and texts.

The age of ancient Egypt might have ended thousands of years ago, but everyone agrees that its presence is still in the air. Due to the remaining carvings and written documents of the events, stories, and legends that took place within the kingdom, it is certain that ancient Egypt will never be forgotten.

Here's another book by Enthralling History that you might like

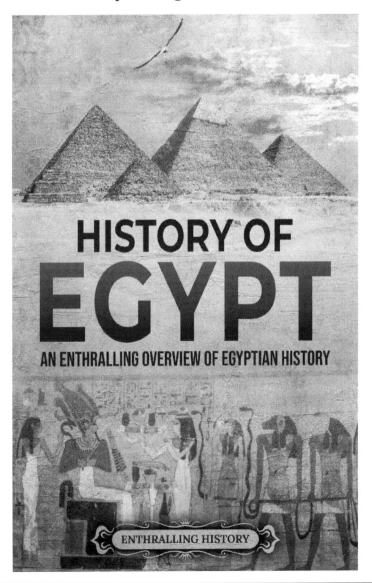

HISTORY OF
EGYPT

AN ENTHRALLING OVERVIEW OF EGYPTIAN HISTORY

ENTHRALLING HISTORY

Free limited time bonus

Stop for a moment. We have a free bonus set up for you. The problem is this: we forget 90% of everything that we read after 7 days. Crazy fact, right? Here's the solution: we've created a printable, 1-page pdf summary for this book that you're reading now. All you have to do to get your free pdf summary is to go to the following website: **https://livetolearn.lpages.co/enthrallinghistory/**

Once you do, it will be intuitive. Enjoy, and thank you!

We forget 90% of everything
that we've read in 7 days...

Get the free printable pdf summary of
the book you've read AND much, much
more... shhhh...

Enter Your Most Frequently Used Email to Get Started

DOWNLOAD FREE PDF
SUMMARY

© Enthralling History

Bibliography

Calvert, A. (n.d.). Old Kingdom and First Intermediate Period, an introduction – Smarthistory. https://smarthistory.org/old-kingdom-first-intermediate-period-introduction/

Edfu Temple - Greco-Roman Period Monuments. (n.d.). https://egyptianmuseum.org/explore/greco-and-roman-period-monuments-edfu-temple

Egypt, Egyptian art during the Ptolemaic Period of Egyptian history | Antiquities Experts. (n.d.). https://www.antiquitiesexperts.com/egypt_ptol.html

Egypt: Piye and the 25th Dynasty. (n.d.). http://www.touregypt.net/featurestories/piye.htm

Egyptian Mummies. (n.d.). Smithsonian Institution. https://www.si.edu/spotlight/ancient-egypt/mummies

Freed, Rita E. *Egypt's Golden Age: The Art of Living in the New Kingdom, 1558-1085 B.C.* Boston: Museum of Fine Arts; 1981.

Heart Scarab | Ancient Egypt Online. (n.d.). https://ancientegyptonline.co.uk/heartscarab/

Herodotus. *The Histories (Penguin Classics Deluxe Edition)*. New York: Penguin Classics; May 19, 2015.

History.com Editors. (2020, November 24). Alexander the Great. HISTORY. https://www.history.com/.amp/topics/ancient-history/alexander-the-great

Ian Shaw. *The Oxford History of Ancient Egypt (Oxford Illustrated History)*. New York: Oxford University Press; October 23, 2003.

J. G. Manning. *The Last Pharaohs: Egypt Under the Ptolemies, 305–30 BC.* Princeton: Princeton University Press; 2009.

King Snefru (Sneferu). (n.d.). https://www.ancient-egypt-online.com/snefru.html

Kinnaer, J. (2014, August 11). Menes | The Ancient Egypt Site. http://www.ancient-egypt.org/who-is-who/m/menes.html

Kitchen, Kenneth Anderson. The Third Intermediate Period in Egypt (1100–650 BC). Warminster: Aris & Phillips Limited; 1996.

Mark, J. J. (2022, November 22). The Great Sphinx of Giza. World History Encyclopedia. https://www.worldhistory.org/Great_Sphinx_of_Giza/

Mark, J. J. (2022, November 23). Djoser. World History Encyclopedia. https://www.worldhistory.org/Djoser/

Mark, J. J. (2022, November 23). Hyksos. World History Encyclopedia. https://www.worldhistory.org/Hyksos/

Mark, J. J. (2022, November 23). The Temple of Hatshepsut. World History Encyclopedia. https://www.worldhistory.org/article/1100/the-temple-of-hatshepsut/

Mark, J. J. (2022, November 24). The Battle of Pelusium: A Victory Decided by Cats. World History Encyclopedia. https://www.worldhistory.org/article/43/the-battle-of-pelusium-a-victory-decided-by-cats/

Mark, J. J. (2022, November 25). Conflict Between the Temple and the Crown in Ancient Egypt. World History Encyclopedia. https://www.worldhistory.org/article/1027/conflict-between-the-temple-and-the-crown-in-ancie/

Mark, J. J. (2022, October 3). Narmer. World History Encyclopedia. https://www.worldhistory.org/Narmer/

Mark, J. J. (2022, September 26). Fayum. World History Encyclopedia. https://www.worldhistory.org/Fayum/

Memphis Tours. (n.d.). Abu Simbel Temples. https://www.memphistours.com/Egypt/Egypt-Wikis/aswan-attractions/wiki/Abu-Simbel-Temples

Merimde in Egypt. (n.d.). https://www.nemo.nu/ibisportal/0egyptintro/2aegypt/merimde.htm

Miroslav Bárta. *Analyzing Collapse: The Rise and Fall of the Old Kingdom (The AUC History of Ancient Egypt).* The American University in Cairo Press; 30 May 2019.

Nijssen, D. (2022, November 21). Cambyses II. World History Encyclopedia. https://www.worldhistory.org/Cambyses_II/

Old Kingdom Monuments Abu Ghurab. (n.d.). https://egyptianmuseum.org/explore/old-kingdom-monuments-abu-ghurab

Oren, Eliezer D. *The Hyksos: New Historical and Archaeological Perspectives*. University of Pennsylvania Museum of Archaeology and Anthropology Philadelphia; 1997.

R.B. Parkinson. *Poetry and Culture in Middle Kingdom Egypt: A Dark Side to Perfection (Studies in Egyptology & the Ancient Near East)*. Equinox Publishing Ltd; 1 Nov. 2010.

Rattini, K. B. (2021, May 3). Pharaoh Ahmose I—facts and information. Culture. https://www.nationalgeographic.com/culture/article/ahmose-i

Rattini, K. B. (2021, May 4). Cyrus the Great: History's most merciful conqueror? Culture. https://www.nationalgeographic.com/culture/article/cyrus-the-great

Roberto B. Gozzoli. *The Writing of History in Ancient Egypt During the First Millennium BCE (ca. 1070–180 BCE): Trends and Perspectives*. London: Golden House Publications; 2006.

Ryan, D. P. (2021). *24 Hours in Ancient Egypt: A Day in the Life of the People Who Lived There*. Adfo Books.

Ryholt, Kim. *The Political Situation in Egypt during the Second Intermediate Period c. 1800–1550 B.C.* Museum Tuscalanum Press; 1997.

Sculpture of the Old Kingdom. (n.d.). http://kolibri.teacherinabox.org.au/modules/en-boundless/

The Pyramids of the Middle Empire. (n.d.). https://www.wonders-of-the-world.net/Pyramids-of-Egypt/Pyramids-of-the-middle-empire.php

Thomas, Angela P. Akhenaten's Egypt. Shire Egyptology 10. Princes Risborough, UK Shire; 1988.

Bingen, Jean. Hellenistic Egypt: Monarchy, Society, Economy, Culture. Berkeley University of California Press; 2007.

Toby Wilkinson. *The Rise and Fall of Ancient Egypt*. United States: Random House; January 8, 2013.

Wasson, D. L. (2022, August 31). Ptolemy I. World History Encyclopedia. https://www.worldhistory.org/Ptolemy_I/

Wasson, D. L. (2022, November 22). Battle of Issus. World History Encyclopedia. https://www.worldhistory.org/Battle_of_Issus/

Wikipedia contributors. (2022, May 19). Ka statue. Wikipedia. https://en.wikipedia.org/wiki/Ka_statue

Wikipedia contributors. (2022, November 10). Book of the Dead. Wikipedia. https://en.wikipedia.org/wiki/Book_of_the_Dead

Wikipedia contributors. (2022, November 15). Prehistoric Egypt. Wikipedia. https://en.wikipedia.org/wiki/Prehistoric_Egypt

Wikipedia contributors. (2022, September 10). Achaemenid conquest of Egypt. Wikipedia. https://en.wikipedia.org/wiki/Achaemenid_conquest_of_Egypt

Wolfram Grajetzki. *The Middle Kingdom of Ancient Egypt: History, Archaeology and Society (Duckworth Egyptology Illustrated Edition)*. London: Bristol Classical Press; 24 Feb. 2006.

Printed in Poland
by Amazon Fulfillment
Poland Sp. z o.o., Wrocław
10 July 2023

7ad6a4d3-8af7-41c8-bb4e-8d3f733306b8R01